Censorship

Other Books in the Current Controversies Series:

Censorship

Laura K. Egendorf, *Book Editor*

David Bender, *Publisher*
Bruno Leone, *Executive Editor*

Bonnie Szumski, *Editorial Director*
Stuart B. Miller, *Managing Editor*

CURRENT CONTROVERSIES

Cover photo: ©1999 Rommel Pecson/Impact Visuals

Library of Congress Cataloging-in-Publication Data

Censorship / Laura K. Egendorf, book editor.
    p. cm. — (Current controversies)
    Includes bibliographical references and index.
    ISBN 0-7377-0450-0 (lib. bdg. : alk. paper) — ISBN 0-7377-0449-7 (pbk. : alk. paper)
    1. Censorship. I. Egendorf, Laura K., 1973–   II. Series.

Z657 .C39   2001
363.3'1—dc21
    00-037672
    CIP

©2001 by Greenhaven Press, Inc., PO Box 289009, San Diego, CA 92198-9009
Printed in the U.S.A.

Contents

needed to ensure that flag burning, hate speech, and other controversial
types of expression receive the protection to which they are entitled.

Chapter 2: Does Censorship Occur in the Educational System?

Yes: Censorship Exists in the Educational System

the courts have sought to protect the teaching of evolution, some school boards are compelling their teachers to teach creationism and discredit evolution.

No: Restrictions of Speech in the Educational System Is Not Censorship

Chapter 3: Should Pornography Be Censored?

Yes: Pornography Should Be Censored

Chapter 4: Should the Government Regulate Art and Popular Culture?

albums with violent or sexually explicit lyrics so that parents can be aware of albums that might be inappropriate for their children.

The music industry has done a poor job of ensuring that violent and offensive music is not sold to children. Parents need information so they can properly determine what music is appropriate for their children.

Foreword

By definition, controversies are "discussions of questions in which opposing opinions clash" (Webster's Twentieth Century Dictionary Unabridged). Few would deny that controversies are a pervasive part of the human condition and exist on virtually every level of human enterprise. Controversies transpire between individuals and among groups, within nations and between nations. Controversies supply the grist necessary for progress by providing challenges and challengers to the status quo. They also create atmospheres where strife and warfare can flourish. A world without controversies would be a peaceful world; but it also would be, by and large, static and prosaic.

The Series' Purpose

The purpose of the Current Controversies series is to explore many of the social, political, and economic controversies dominating the national and international scenes today. Titles selected for inclusion in the series are highly focused and specific. For example, from the larger category of criminal justice, Current Controversies deals with specific topics such as police brutality, gun control, white collar crime, and others. The debates in Current Controversies also are presented in a useful, timeless fashion. Articles and book excerpts included in each title are selected if they contribute valuable, long-range ideas to the overall debate. And wherever possible, current information is enhanced with historical documents and other relevant materials. Thus, while individual titles are current in focus, every effort is made to ensure that they will not become quickly outdated. Books in the Current Controversies series will remain important resources for librarians, teachers, and students for many years.

In addition to keeping the titles focused and specific, great care is taken in the editorial format of each book in the series. Book introductions and chapter prefaces are offered to provide background material for readers. Chapters are organized around several key questions that are answered with diverse opinions representing all points on the political spectrum. Materials in each chapter include opinions in which authors clearly disagree as well as alternative opinions in which authors may agree on a broader issue but disagree on the possible solutions. In this way, the content of each volume in Current Controversies mirrors the mosaic of opinions encountered in society. Readers will quickly realize that there are many viable answers to these complex issues. By questioning each author's conclusions, students and casual readers can begin to develop the critical thinking skills so important to evaluating opinionated material.

Current Controversies is also ideal for controlled research. Each anthology in the series is composed of primary sources taken from a wide gamut of informational categories including periodicals, newspapers, books, United States and foreign government documents, and the publications of private and public organizations. Readers will find factual support for reports, debates, and research papers covering all areas of important issues. In addition, an annotated table of contents, an index, a book and periodical bibliography, and a list of organizations to contact are included in each book to expedite further research.

Perhaps more than ever before in history, people are confronted with diverse and contradictory information. During the Persian Gulf War, for example, the public was not only treated to minute-to-minute coverage of the war, it was also inundated with critiques of the coverage and countless analyses of the factors motivating U.S. involvement. Being able to sort through the plethora of opinions accompanying today's major issues, and to draw one's own conclusions, can be a complicated and frustrating struggle. It is the editors' hope that Current Controversies will help readers with this struggle.

Greenhaven Press anthologies primarily consist of previously published material taken from a variety of sources, including periodicals, books, scholarly journals, newspapers, government documents, and position papers from private and public organizations. These original sources are often edited for length and to ensure their accessibility for a young adult audience. The anthology editors also change the original titles of these works in order to clearly present the main thesis of each viewpoint and to explicitly indicate the opinion presented in the viewpoint. These alterations are made in consideration of both the reading and comprehension levels of a young adult audience. Every effort is made to ensure that Greenhaven Press accurately reflects the original intent of the authors included in this anthology.

"The issues raised by the [Communications Decency Act]—such as whether the government can restrict speech and what role the government should play in censoring material to protect children— are relevant to the debate over censorship as a whole."

Introduction

The writer A.J. Liebling once said: "Freedom of the press is guaranteed only to those who own one." With the advent of the Internet, however, this is no longer the case—anyone with a computer and Internet access can create a website or post their views on virtually any topic. While many websites provide useful and factual information, others contain pornographic material. These sites are sometimes included in the results of searches on innocuous terms such as "toys" or "teenagers." Furthermore, some porn sites use web addresses that give no indication as to the content of the material, which can lead Internet users to enter those sites by mistake. Consequently, some people have expressed concern that children will be exposed to sexually explicit or violent material while using the Internet. In response to these fears, President Bill Clinton signed into law the Communications Decency Act of 1996. The CDA, part of 1996's Telecommunications Act, sought to reduce children's access to pornography by imposing prison terms and fines on people who spread obscene material over the Internet.

Not surprisingly, civil liberties organizations—which assert that even potentially offensive speech must be permitted—and computer companies soon challenged the law. In June 1996, in the case of *ACLU v. Reno*, a special federal court panel ruled that the CDA infringed on the First Amendment and therefore could not be enforced. The following year, the Supreme Court overturned the CDA on a 7–2 vote. However, the issues raised by the CDA—such as whether the government can restrict speech and what role the government should play in censoring material to protect children—are relevant to the debate over censorship as a whole.

The federal court gave several reasons as to why the CDA could not be put into action. It contended that the CDA violated the First Amendment because the act's vague and overly broad provisions made it unclear as to what speech might be considered inappropriate to transmit over the Internet; hence, websites that disseminate information about AIDS or reproduction could be considered indecent. The court also maintained that government proposals to ensure that only adults would be able to access sexually explicit sites are not feasible, because it is impossible to verify a user's age over the

Internet. According to federal court judge Dolores Sloviter:

> Whatever the strength of the interest the government has demonstrated in preventing minors from accessing "indecent" and "patently offensive" material online, if the means it has chosen sweeps more broadly than necessary and thereby chills the expression of adults, it has overstepped onto rights protected by the First Amendment.

One argument frequently presented against censorship is that parents can determine what books, television programs, or websites are appropriate for their children and do not need government initiatives such as the CDA or the V-chip (a device installed in televisions so parents can prevent their children from watching certain programs). In "Beyond the Communications Decency Act: Constitutional Lessons of the Internet," Solveig Bernstein, then assistant director of telecommunications and technology studies at the Cato Institute, a libertarian public policy research institution, claims: "It is not rational to argue . . . that government can have a compelling interest in helping concerned parents when concerned parents do not need help." Bernstein contends that should parents want help in limiting their children's access to the Internet, they can turn to private companies who offer filtering software. She maintains that these programs are effective and affordable. Bernstein also notes that some parents might not choose to limit access, believing that "their children should be exposed to materials that might be considered indecent, including information about disease prevention, birth control, . . . and so on."

Supporters of the CDA and other efforts by the government to keep minors from accessing sexually explicit material, in contrast, contend that restricting such speech does not violate the Constitution. According to the Clinton administration, in a brief submitted in *ACLU v. Reno*, the CDA is "the latest in a long line of congressional efforts to protect children from exposure to indecent material." Such efforts have included regulating access by minors to "dial-a-porn" and some cable channels. The brief also states that the CDA does not violate the First Amendment because, "indecent communications have such little social value that they are at the bottom of the scale of protected speech." Proving the adage that "politics make strange bedfellows," the Clinton White House's views were supported by many conservative writers and organizations, who agreed with the CDA and expressed dismay at the Supreme Court's ruling. Conservative columnist William H. Buckley Jr. wrote in the *National Review*: "My own judgment of the Internet is that it is the most exciting technological research and information tool of the century, but this has nothing to do at all with the challenge of ensuring that only adults would have access to its darker corners." Groups such as Enough is Enough, an anti-pornography organization, and the National League of Cities, also stated their disappointment in the ruling. Countering the argument that government should have no say in how parents allow their children to use the Internet, NLC's Public Safety and Crime Prevention chairman Hal Daub states: "While parents will always have the ultimate responsibility for protecting their children, government should help provide them the tools to do that in areas where the parents have little access and control, such as with the Internet." In addition, Gerald Damschen, the webmaster of the Original Responsible Speech Page, maintains that the CDA's restrictions on minors' access to websites are no different than those barring youth from adult movies. He asserts that free speech is a right that must be used responsibly.

The debate over the Communications Decency Act is merely one of the more recent censorship controversies. As long as people write books or create art, there will be disagreement over whether the government has the right to censor those works. These and related arguments are the subject of *Censorship: Current Controversies*. In this book, the authors examine whether censorship in the educational system, the mass media, or art and popular culture is ever necessary.

Chapter 1

Should Speech Be Censored?

Chapter Preface

In December 1999, *Sports Illustrated* published an interview with Atlanta Braves relief pitcher John Rocker. In the article, Rocker insulted the driving skills of Asian women, referred to a teammate, in a presumably racial comment, as a "fat monkey," and noted that he disliked New York City because of the preponderance of foreigners and subway cars filled with "some kid with purple hair next to some queer with AIDS." Rocker's statements are an example of what many people consider to be the problem of hate speech.

Hate speech is speech that encourages prejudice, and sometimes violence, toward specific groups, due to race, sexual orientation, gender, or other factors. The Supreme Court has heard several hate speech cases over the past six decades. In 1952, the court considered *Beauharnais v. Illinois*, which involved a man who led a white supremacist organization and had distributed leaflets containing racist comments and threats toward African Americans. The court ruled that "group libel"—defamatory speech directed at a group of people—should be restricted. In cases in the 1980s and 1990s, however, the court has ruled that restrictions on hate speech, such as speech codes at state universities, are unconstitutional. Private entities can restrict hate speech, however; for example, Major League Baseball fined and suspended Rocker.

Despite the court rulings, many people assert that restrictions on hate speech are necessary because such speech is demeaning and creates uncomfortable campuses and workplaces. Richard Delgado, a law professor at the University of Colorado, maintains that hate speech laws have been successful in other countries. He writes: "A host of Western democracies have instituted laws against hate speech and crime. . . . In none has there been a noticeable erosion of the spirit of free inquiry."

However, some commentators have argued that Rocker and others have the right to express their views—even if those views may be considered hateful. Stephen M. Nichols, a political science professor, writes: "A society that values free speech must tolerate even offensive speech." Some analysts also claim that offensive speech should not be censored but instead responded to by more speech. Columnist Cal Thomas observes: "The response to outrageous speech ought not to be silencing the speaker, but the encouragement of more speech. A fool does himself in when he keeps speaking rubbish."

The John Rocker controversy is an example of the debate on whether any speech should be censored. In the following chapter, the authors consider whether all speech should be free and protected or if censorship is justified under certain situations.

Censorship Is Necessary

by David Lowenthal

About the author: *David Lowenthal is a professor emeritus of political science at Boston College and the author of* No Liberty for License: The Forgotten Logic of the First Amendment.

On July 21, 1999, a distinguished group of citizens released "An Appeal to Hollywood." Among the 56 signers were William Bennett, Jimmy Carter, Mario Cuomo, Richard John Neuhaus, Colin Powell, Norman Schwarzkopf, Elie Wiesel, and James Q. Wilson. Concerned about "an increasingly toxic popular culture" and spurred by the [April 1999] high school shootings in Littleton, Colorado, these eminent Americans called on the producers and sponsors of mass entertainment to "take modest steps of self-restraint" to make television, movies, and music less violent and lewd. What they explicitly declined to recommend was government censorship.

Steve Allen's Efforts

The previous fall, the first of the signatories, Steve Allen, had formed an organization called Parents Television Council and taken out full-page ads across the country proclaiming, "TV Is Leading Children Down a Moral Sewer: How You and I Can Stop It." The council's object was to close up the sewer by putting heavy pressure on the sponsors of television shows. The July 21 appeal constitutes a significant further step in the same direction. It is impressive, and encouraging, to see so many who have served their country well, in so many walks of life, doff political partisanship and give united public voice to their dismay and their hope.

I joined Allen's council as soon as I saw his daring ad, but I did so without any confidence that his plan to influence sponsors would succeed. Nor am I sanguine about the "Appeal to Hollywood." There have been many such appeals before. Steadily, things have gotten worse. Hollywood, constituting one of the country's most powerful establishment industries, seems equally enamored of its profits and its artistic pretensions. There is no sign of its intending to respond to the fears of parents for their children and of citizens for the republic.

Reprinted from David Lowenthal, "The Case for Censorship," *The Weekly Standard*, August 23, 1999. Reprinted with permission from *The Weekly Standard*. For more information on subscribing to *The Weekly Standard*, please call 1-800-283-2014 or visit the website www.weeklystandard.com.

At most, the industry, wrapping itself in the First Amendment, reshuffles its movie-rating labels and continues its descent. Far more effective than the appeal's polite request for "modest steps of self-restraint" by the industry would be strong, meaningful threats, followed by state and national legislation. In this more vigorous course, censorship has an important place.

The case for regulating the mass media today rests on several premises: that the mass media are the prime educational force in the country; that their effect is, by and large, pernicious—running counter to the education of the young in schools, churches, and synagogues and to the qualities required of mature citizens in a civilized republic; and that government, and government alone, has a chance of blocking this descent into decadence. The argument to be overcome is that censorship is dangerous, ineffective, unconstitutional, and inconsistent with liberal democracy.

The Moral Pollution of Mass Media

The mass media include television, the movies, and recordings, but the term can be extended to cover popular books and magazines and, now, the Internet as well. The present discussion concentrates on the first three media. There are a few people who regard television and the movies as mere entertainment. Their view is that what we see and hear with such frequency is like water off a duck's back: We are amused, moved, or entranced without being affected. Censorship is not for them. Those, however, who consider the influence of the mass media actual and malignant will seek some recourse. Censorship or, more broadly, regulation, is the needed recourse—one we have been prevented from considering by a combination of Supreme Court enthusiasts and the mass media themselves.

As a nation we are concerned about pollution, about pure air and water, about every aspect of the physical environment, about the prevention and cure of disease in all its forms. Is there no such thing as moral pollution? Has our increasing awareness of the goods and evils of the body been bought at the cost of an increasing dullness regarding the goods and evils of the soul? Are we incapable of recognizing the debilitation that weakens or destroys those qualities that make us distinctively human?

That there is cause for concern about the media is recognized by thoughtful conservatives and liberals alike. Conservatives are especially sensitive to the sexual immorality the

"The case for regulating the mass media today rests on several premises."

media purvey, liberals to the encouragement of violence. Both are right, as far as they go, but the full picture is even more alarming. Never before in the history of mankind have the moral restraints and aspirations necessary to the fullness of our nature, and to civilization itself, been subjected to so ubiquitous and persistent an assault. If our scientific learning and partisan ideologies keep us from seeing this—from seeing that we are on the road to decadence and decline—of what use are they?

A History of American Censorship

Assuming that enough of the country can still recognize the base and the vicious for what they are, is there anything that can be done to rein in the corruption wrought by the mass media? What can we do to reverse the caninization of the human species occurring before our eyes and retreat from the barbarism it is spawning?

Let us recall some history. When Sir William Blackstone, from whom our Founding Fathers learned most of their law, pioneered the notion of the

> *"Is there no such thing as moral pollution?"*

freedom of the press, his purpose was to free the press from the heavy hand of the censor. At the time, the press simply meant the printing press. Blackstone justified its emancipation from the censors, who were empowered to block the publication of offending material, not by insisting that such offenses go unpunished, but by affirming that they could be adequately punished *after* publication.

Blackstone never questioned what he regarded as a self-evident principle: that no one has a right to use words (or pictures) to inflict serious harm on others or on society. Blackstone called abuses of the press "libels," and among the types he listed were "immoral libels," the forerunner of obscenity. These punishable offenses were considered "license," not an exercise of liberty, and were never protected by the freedom of the press.

Starting near the end of World War I, Justices Oliver Wendell Holmes and Louis Brandeis steered the law away from Blackstone's understanding of press freedom and in the direction of John Stuart Mill's philosophy of extreme liberty. In cases involving left-wing attacks on the draft and on our whole system of government, these justices substituted their own "clear and present danger" test for the prevailing Blackstonian position that the press could not be lawfully used to encourage violence and lawlessness. The test meant that government had to wait until law-breaking was imminent before it could act against the use of the press to promote it. By the middle of the century, this new principle had gained acceptance on the Court for revolutionary speech and press and was beginning to extend the limits of sexual expression as well. It seemed to offer a more exact way of deciding when government could act against the misuse of the press. What it lacked was prudence.

Dangers can be real and still not offer "clear and present" threats to individuals. Is fanning the flames of selfish and irresponsible lust, as obscenity does, not dangerous to our society? How can we expect the sexes to treat each other with decency and respect, the very young to forbear from sexual intercourse, and the family to remain stable in mutual devotion if sex detached from any sense of responsibility and even from love is touted daily in theaters and on television screens? Is it unreasonable to believe that an important cause of the instability of the American family today, and of our enormous rate of illegitimacy, is the climate of sexual laxity encouraged by movie after movie, show after show?

The Obscenity Confusion

From early in our history, obscenity has been a crime in every state in the nation, and this is perfectly consistent with the freedom of speech and of the press guaranteed in our state and federal constitutions. Obscenity has never been protected by the First Amendment. But starting in 1957 (with *Roth v. United States*), the Supreme Court's view of obscenity began to change. We need not review here the ins and outs of the Court's interpretations. The result, by 1973 (in *Miller v. California*), was to narrow the legal definition of obscenity to pornography, thus discouraging the prosecution of any appeal to lust short of the display of sexual organs and acts. Even the prosecution of pornography has been rendered dispirited: In our progressive age, enforcement of the laws against obscenity is out of fashion.

In recent years the Court has gone so far as to insist that "indecent" material be given its share of viewing hours on television. And, although the Court eventually decided the standard prohibition of obscenity must apply to the Internet, cyberspace has become an unequaled global showcase for pornography. A single illustration of how the Court's 1973 interpretation of obscenity works in practice tells it all. In the lower courts, the manifestly obscene lyrics of the rap group 2 Live Crew, with their explicit incitement to violence against women, were accorded First Amendment protection, in deference to their "serious value," attested to by so-called experts.

You don't have to be a member of the Christian Right to realize that something is wrong here. In a word, the Supreme Court, the law schools, and like-minded opinion leaders have replaced the thought of the Founders and Framers with a radical understanding of individual liberty, incoherently mixed with the morally corrosive relativism of the mid-twentieth century. Pressed by secular intellectuals to liberate ourselves from Victorian prudery, we have thrown off all restraints, imagining that we can satisfy all natural appetites while remaining civilized and free.

> *"From early in our history, obscenity has been a crime in every state in the nation."*

The mass media—the movies, television, and recordings—need to be regulated, and not only because of appeals to irresponsible lust. They have immersed us in violence as well, habituated us to the most extreme brutality, held it up as a model and surrounded us by images of hateful human types so memorable as to cause a psychological insecurity that is dangerous. The only answer is governmental regulation, if necessary prior to publication—that is, censorship.

Chapter 1

Questions to Consider

We must now face these questions: (a) Is not prior restraint, or censorship in the strict sense, banned by the very idea of the freedom of the press? Would censorship of the movies, television, and recordings be constitutional? (b) Can censorship be made responsible and consistent with the needs of republican government? Why should what we see and hear be determined by some faceless bureaucrat? Will censorship not be misused and abused by politicians? (c) Is censorship enough to correct the moral corruption that has already shown itself in our midst?

It is true that freedom of the press originally meant the elimination of censorship. But the abuses of "the press" as then understood—books, pamphlets, handbills—could be corrected by punishment subsequent to publication. The offending materials, which in any case circulated slowly, could be withdrawn from circulation. By contrast, the movies, television, and recordings can be "published" at once all over the country, to be seen and heard by millions, young and old alike. That is what makes them mass media. Furthermore, the visual and auditory appeal of drama and music gives them a power totally different from that of printed matter. Equating these media with the press in its exact sense is like calling atomic missiles artillery.

> *"The harm caused by movies and television programs shown even once can be widespread and serious."*

We cannot be sure that the first stout defenders of the press, like Blackstone and John Milton (who also favored post-publication punishment for abuses of the press) would make an exception for movies and television were they alive today. But their principle requires it, for they assume that serious harm to the public by the use of words or pictures is to be prohibited; the manner of accomplishing this is secondary. The harm caused by printed material can be minimized after publication, but the harm caused by movies and television programs shown even once can be widespread and serious.

As to our constitutional tradition, the Supreme Court has never closed the door to prior restraint in the case of movies, though it has (in *Freedman v. Maryland,* 1965, and *Southeastern Promotions, Ltd. v. Conrad,* 1975) imposed on state and local censorship boards procedural burdens so great as to render them inoperative. The Court has forgotten what Chief Justice Charles Evans Hughes said as far back as 1931, in a landmark case prohibiting the prior restraint of newspapers (*Near v. Minnesota*). He listed four specific abuses of the press in connection with which the First Amendment would allow even prior restraint. Notably, he stated that "the primary requirements of decency may be enforced against obscene publications." How much more would this exception allowing prior restraint apply to the powerful force the movies are today.

The case of television is different again. Broadcast stations or bands of airwaves are a public property allocated with conditions attached. In the Federal Communications Act of 1934, it was stipulated that programming had to be in the "public interest"—a basic condition Congress failed to amplify on then or since. But the principle is there, ready to be spelled out in the future. If the conditions for obtaining and renewing licenses are made plain and then applied consistently, there should be little need for the prior screening of individual programs.

The Best Approach to Censorship

Who will do the censoring? In monarchical days of old, the censor was an individual appointed by the king. From his secret decisions there was no appeal. In our own experience, there were boards of censors as well as individual censors in many of our states and cities whose main business was to supervise movies and shows like burlesques. Even today their vestigial remains can be found here and there. But for the most part, they were driven out of existence in the 1970s and '80s not because they were suddenly deemed intrinsically unconstitutional, but because the Supreme Court placed increasing restrictions on them, at the same time that it reduced the scope of state authority in dealing with the harm done by the movies. In 1959, for example, a case came before the Court (*Kingsley International Pictures Corp. v. Regents*) involving the refusal of New York State's Board of Regents to allow the showing of the movie *Lady Chatterley's Lover.* The board maintained that the movie gave encouragement to adultery. Brandishing its Mill-derived version of the First Amendment, the Court countered that even such encouragement, like all "ideas," was protected by the freedom of the press.

Formerly the censors, often appointed, were relatively unknown individuals. Today, it should be possible to enlist some of our most distinguished citizens— like those signing the July 21 "Appeal to Hollywood"—to serve as censors, now that we realize, as before we did not, how central, rather than peripheral, this function really is. In our almost fastidious legal system, their decisions— unlike those of the censors of old—would be guided by law, open to inspection, and subject to review by higher courts. Could their power be abused? Of course it could. It could also be eluded by those who will seek every way they can to thrust their innovations on an unwitting public.

The Moral State of America

But a graver question is whether enough is left of our moral character and understanding as a nation to allow us to frame and apply laws that will curb the most baneful aspects of the mass media. No one knows. The picture of America we see on television is not necessarily an accurate depiction of our urban and rural heartlands. And while our moral corruption has other sources, including excessive wealth, the mass media, which propagate the ideas and images we use to picture ourselves, are the most obvious and most important. A sick man is often helped through his illness by his will to prevail, as well as by the measures taken to make him well. Recourse to a reasonable but rigorous system of censorship will signify that the country understands what has happened and is determined to survive as a civilized and free society.

As for the final complaint—"I don't want anybody telling me what I can and can't see"—the answer is simple: That is exactly our situation now, where a few hidden figures in movie studios and television networks, motivated primarily by profit, decide what will be available for our viewing. With few exceptions, the viewer is offered a variety of bad alternatives, whatever their technical wizardry, for inch by inch, yard by yard, the mass media have lowered the standards of their productions, appealing increasingly to animal appetites that, once released, give little quarter to the nobler elements of freedom and civilization.

> *"The choice is clear: either a rigorous censorship of the mass media . . . or an accelerating descent into barbarism."*

The choice is clear: either a rigorous censorship of the mass media, in conformity with responsible republican government, with censors known to all and operating under law, or an accelerating descent into barbarism and the destruction, sooner or later, of free society itself.

Hate Speech Should Be Outlawed

by Terrie Albano

About the author: *Terrie Albano is a member of the national board of the Communist Party.*

Communists are in a unique position to discuss free speech and hate groups. Our unique position comes from our militant history of being in the forefront of free speech fights—from Elizabeth Gurley Flynn as a founder of the ACLU protecting and expanding free speech for workers and their organizations, to fights demanding Paul Robeson have the right to speak and perform, to Gus Hall and the Berkeley Free Speech Movement. Our party has been on the cutting edge of developing and deepening the democratic ideal of free speech by fighting to extend it to the whole working class.

Communists are also in a unique position because Communist Party members were in the most unfortunate and undemocratic position of being denied their freedom of speech. During one of the most undemocratic periods in our country's history, the Cold War McCarthy period, communists—based on lies, trumped-up charges and witch-hunt hysteria—were victims of the government legally suppressing their freedom of speech. Worse than that, leaders of the Communist Party were jailed for "conspiracy to teach." They were jailed for their beliefs and thoughts!

An Unequal Right to Free Speech

So when the FBI gets on "Nightline," as it did in the wake of the anti-Semitic and racist shootings and murder in California, and defends the rights of individuals to their beliefs, it is clear that the beliefs of racists and Nazis will be defended by the FBI, but the beliefs of Communists, progressives, trade unionists, peace and civil rights activists will not be.

Like all things, democracy and free speech have a class basis. There is freedom for the ruling class and corporate interests, whose bottom line is maximum

Reprinted from Terrie Albano, "On Free Speech and Hate Groups," *People's Weekly World*, August 21, 1999. Reprinted with permission from the author.

profit and exploitation, and restrictions for the victims of exploitation and those who challenge it.

There may be free speech for bigots, but not free speech for workers trying to organize a union—those workers get fired, black-listed or run out of town.

There may be free speech for Nazis and the Klan, but not free speech for strikers fighting the good fight—the courts hand down anti-picket injunctions preventing strikers from assembling.

There may be free speech for racists advocating police "racial profiling," but not free speech for victims of racism, police harassment and brutality. The victims are slandered and convicted either by the police being judge, jury and executioner or by the mass media in their court of racist coverage.

Violent Threats Are Not Free Speech

Free speech has a class line. It also has a class responsibility. One person's beliefs cannot cross the line into threats of violence. Free speech does not cover that. Those kinds of terrorist acts threaten everyone's free speech. It creates a chilling effect on public discussion when the hate mongers call for killing based on race, national origin, religion, who one loves or whether you provide or seek a legal medical procedure. It is only in the ruling class and corporate interests that these terrorist groups are allowed to exist.

> *"One person's beliefs cannot cross the line into threats of violence. Free speech does not cover that."*

That's why not allowing the Klan to march or jailing White Aryan Resistance leader, Tom Metzger, for his public calls for violence is not a violation of freedom of speech. Those acts will, in fact, deepen and broaden freedom of speech by "de-terrorizing" the atmosphere.

The Communist Party constantly gets letters, calls and e-mail from thousands across the country who are intimidated by these forces and can't speak their views and organize according to their beliefs because of the terrorist ultra-right groups, be it militia or neo-Nazi, because of the atmosphere they create. This atmosphere of fear is a direct assault on freedom of speech.

The majority of American people are seeing this class divide. It is evident in the majority opinion in favor of hate crimes legislation. It is evident by the majority opinion against violence and hate speech based on race, nationality, status, sexual orientation or religion.

Hate Groups Must Be Outlawed

It is in the interests of the overwhelming majority in our country to outlaw groups of racism, hate and terror. In the name of human decency and democracy their existence cannot be allowed to continue. The government knows who these groups are but it's up to a united coalition of white, black, Latino, Asian, American Indian, Pacific Islander, Middle Eastern, men and women, gay and straight, Jewish, Christian, Muslim, Buddhist, Hindu and atheist, immigrant and U.S.-born, and people's organizations—trade unions, civil rights, religious, peace, women's and elected officials to struggle and force the government to act.

Does outlawing racist, anti-Semitic, bigoted hate groups make racism or bigotry go away? No. But it is a giant step in democratizing public discourse and free speech. And it is a giant step in making all our lives and the lives of our children safer.

Flag Burning Should Be Banned

by Armstrong Williams

About the author: *Armstrong Williams is a nationally syndicated columnist.*

The freedom of speech, as guaranteed by the First Amendment, while often threatened, has withstood the assaults of those who would seek to deny it to us. It has proved to be one of our most important freedoms, but we must maintain constant vigilance that neither is it abused. Flag burning is a lurid abuse of that right. Moreover, it is alarming that one of our most cherished freedoms would be used to protect the desecration of our flag.

Debating the First Amendment

The exact nature of the First Amendment and what types of speech it protects has been argued ever since the adoption of the Constitution. Perhaps no other section of that great document has excited so much debate. Even today, there is still disagreement. Does it cover acts such as flag burning? Just what does it cover?

The Constitution states that "Congress shall make no law," but it says nothing about what states may do. In the 1964 case, *The New York Times v. Sullivan,* the Supreme Court ruled that states could not bar free speech any more than the federal government. This maintained the supremacy of the Constitution, which guarantees the rights of *all* citizens. It is the law of the land, superseding state and local statutes.

Congress passed the Sedition Act in 1798, making it a crime to "write, print, utter or publish" anything negative about the government with intent to defame, or incite contempt or hatred of Congress or the president. At the time, it was deemed necessary to protect the government from a riotous public. It was a disaster, and Thomas Jefferson revoked the law when he took office in 1801.

Can you imagine if such a law existed today? Our country would be in chaos. I think it is safe to say that our fledgling nation would not have survived. Certainly, it would be a far different world today had that law been allowed to stand.

Reprinted from Armstrong Williams, "Conduct Unbecoming Free Speech," *The American Legion Magazine*, July 1998. Reprinted with permission from the author.

Threats to our freedoms did not end there. Our history has been a struggle to guarantee to all Americans those inalienable rights with which we have been endowed by our Creator.

America is the land of the free, but that freedom has not come easy. Many are still denied the same freedoms most of us take for granted. Without the guarantee of our Constitution, we would be a sorry lot, afraid to do or say anything that might remotely cause harm to any group or individual. It is doubtful we would be the greatest nation in the world today if we were without that noble document. It puts into words our beliefs as Americans.

The American Flag Is a Symbol

The U.S. Flag is another essential and powerful symbol of our great nation. It represents the strength of our unity and embodies the spirit of the phrase: "e pluribus unum." The Stars and Stripes symbolizes liberty, too. America is the "land of the free and the home of the brave," many of whom fought and died for their beloved country. These patriots did not sacrifice their lives so that others might abuse their God-given freedoms.

Many people feel it is their right to criticize and challenge authority. The right to rebel has been respected by philosophers, writers and other thinkers for centuries. They ask: Are we to deny ourselves and others that right and become simple and unthinking subjects of our government? No! We are not powerless subjects of an exclusive and insular regime. We, the people, are the source of authority, which is the basis of democracy.

> *"While free speech is one of the four freedoms protected by the First Amendment, it cannot be applied to flag burning."*

There is, however, a distinction to be drawn between constructive criticism and destructive opposition. Discourse on our particular brand of democracy should never aim to weaken our system of government. The goal of dialogue is to improve and build, not tear down; to move forward and not regress.

While free speech is one of the four freedoms protected by the First Amendment, it cannot be applied to flag burning. It is different from speech in that no words are spoken and nothing is written. It is a destructive act of disloyalty and should never be protected as a right. No part of the Constitution, however loosely interpreted, can be used to defend such conduct.

Timothy McVeigh blew up the Alfred Murrah Federal Building in Oklahoma City out of anger to protest the government's action against the Branch Davidians in Waco, Texas. He was wrong to use violence. If citizens are dissatisfied or upset with government policy, there are many other peaceful, nondestructive avenues to make your grievances known.

Ted Kaczynski felt threatened by what he perceived to be the growing and unregulated power of technology and also reacted violently, sending letter bombs to those who he felt in some way symbolized what he feared. Such behavior, however rationalized, cannot be tolerated. As citizens of the United States of America, we all must respect and follow the same laws and rules of conduct.

Destruction Is Not a Right

An act of destruction can never be protected as a natural and legal right. That is why it is so important for us to pass an amendment to the Constitution to protect the U.S. Flag from those who would desecrate it. The argument that the act of flag burning is protected under the First Amendment is ill-founded and mistaken. No one can argue that conduct is the same as speech. As we protect the one, we also must ensure the other is not abused.

An amendment to protect our national symbol—the U.S. Flag—is not only necessary, it is the moral thing to do. To stand idly by and allow the desecration of our flag is an outrage, and most Americans will not—should not—tolerate such behavior. All citizens who truly love their country should support protecting our flag from malicious destruction.

An amendment to protect the flag is not a drastic move and will not endanger our rights. It will not curtail our right to free speech, as some claim, because physical desecration is an act—a destructive act that cannot logically be protected under the mantle of free speech.

George Washington believed that the Constitution was made more perfect each time it was amended. The first 10 amendments greatly improved that document. Yet, they seemed to raise as many questions as they answered. Thomas Jefferson, in his inaugural address on March 4, 1801, offered to let all those with whom we disagree "stand undisturbed as monuments of the safety with which error of opinion may be tolerated where reason is left free to combat it." That might be true when it comes to speaking one's mind, but desecration of our nation's flag cannot "stand undisturbed." The way to protect Old Glory is through a constitutional amendment, and the U.S. Senate should listen to the majority of Americans who support it. It's the right thing to do, and the time is now. [As of January 2000, an amendment on flag burning had not been approved in the Senate or ratified by thirty-eight states.]

Anti-Abortion Protests Can Be Limited

by Gregory K. Scott

About the author: *Gregory K. Scott is a Colorado Supreme Court justice.*

Editor's Note: The following viewpoint is an excerpt from a Colorado Supreme Court decision, Hill v. Thomas, *given on February 16, 1999.*

In this case we must decide whether a legislative enactment designed to protect the privacy rights of citizens entering and leaving Colorado health care facilities unduly burdens the First Amendment rights of other citizens. We conclude that it does not. . . .

While the protections afforded by the First Amendment are broad, they are also not limitless. "The First Amendment does not guarantee the right to communicate one's views at all times and places or in any manner that may be desired." *Heffron v. ISKCON,* 452 U.S. 640, 647 (1981). For example, if restriction of speech is facilitated by a content-neutral statute, "[e]xpression, whether oral or written or symbolized by conduct, is subject to reasonable time, place and manner restrictions." *Clark v. Community for Creative Non-Violence,* 468 U.S. 288, 293 (1984).

Content-Neutral Regulations

Because government cannot favor one idea over another, its regulation of speech must be content-neutral. A statute is content-neutral if it is "'justified without reference to the content of the regulated speech.'" *Ward* [*Ward v. Rock Against Racism*], 491 U.S. at 791 (quoting Community for Creative Non-Violence, 468 U.S. at 295). "A regulation that serves purposes unrelated to the content of expression is deemed neutral, even if it has an incidental effect on some speakers or messages but not others." *Ward,* 491 U.S. at 791. In other words, a restriction on speech is content-neutral if the government makes no attempt to control the content of the speech protected and regulated thereby.

We note that both the trial court and the court of appeals found that section 18-

9-122(3) is content-neutral, and that petitioners do not contend otherwise in this appeal. Further, our review of that section satisfies us that it is, indeed, content-neutral. The restrictions apply equally to all demonstrators, regardless of viewpoint, and the statutory language makes no reference to the content of the speech. Thus, we conclude that section 18-9-122(3) is content-neutral, and, therefore, we shall apply the test announced in *Ward*. [Section 18-9-122(3) is a Colorado law that forbids a person from "knowingly [approaching] another person within eight feet of such a person, unless such other person consents, for the purpose of . . . counseling with such other person in the public way or sidewalk area within a radius of one hundred feet from any entrance door to a health care facility.]

> *"While the protections afforded by the First Amendment are broad, they are also not limitless."*

The *Ward* Ruling

Before applying that standard, however, we first review the Supreme Court's holding in *Ward*. In *Ward,* New York City promulgated what it termed "Use Guidelines" in an attempt to regulate the sound amplification systems used by Rock Against Racism (RAR), an organization sponsoring musical concerts to convey a message on New York City property. RAR in turn filed a successful motion for an injunction against enforcement of particular aspects of the guidelines. RAR also sought damages and a declaratory judgment striking down the guidelines as facially invalid. The district court, applying the three-part test for determining the constitutionality of time, place or manner restrictions, found the guidelines valid. On appeal, the Second Circuit Court of Appeals reversed, based on its conclusion that the city could have used less restrictive means of regulating the volume of RAR's concert.

The Supreme Court reversed the federal appellate court and upheld the constitutionality of the city's regulation of speech. In so doing, the Court utilized a two-part test for determining whether the content-neutral guidelines were constitutional. First, the Court inquired into whether the regulation was "'narrowly tailored to serve a significant governmental interest.'" Here, we note that the Court emphasized that the Second Circuit erred in holding that the regulation had to be "'the least intrusive means' of achieving the desired end." Rather, the Court explained, "our cases quite clearly hold that restrictions on time, place or manner of protected speech are not invalid 'simply because there is some imaginable alternative that might be less burdensome on speech.'" The Court then clarified,

> [l]est any confusion on the point remain, we reaffirm today that a regulation of the time, place, or manner of protected speech must be narrowly tailored to serve the government's legitimate, content-neutral interests but that it need not be the least restrictive or least intrusive means of doing so.

The Court then proceeded to the second, and final, requirement for finding a legislatively imposed restriction on speech constitutional, that the restriction leave ample alternative channels of communication open. Here the Court explained the precise nature of permissible restriction of speech by stating, "[t]hat the city's limitations on volume may reduce to some degree the potential audience for respondent's speech is of no consequence, for there has been no showing that the remaining avenues of communication are inadequate." Thus, absent a showing that the resultant, permissible means of communicating information are inadequate for petitioners to express themselves, section 18-9-122(3) will be deemed to have left open ample alternatives, and therefore, should be upheld as constitutional.

Applying the standard set forth in *Ward* here, we hold that section 18-9-122(3) is a reasonable restriction on the time, place, and manner of petitioners' speech and, therefore, is valid under the First Amendment for the reasons set forth below.

Why the Statute Is Acceptable

First, section 18-9-122(3) is sufficiently narrowly drawn to further a significant government interest. The statute mandates that an individual can only be convicted of criminal conduct under specified circumstances. Specifically, section 18-9-122(3) prohibits an individual from knowingly approaching another person within eight feet: (1) for the purpose of oral protest, counseling, education, leafleting, or displaying a sign to that person; (2) within 100 feet of a health care facility entrance; (3) without that person's consent.

Petitioners contend that section 18-9-122(3) is not narrow because, although the General Assembly declared its intent to curtail threatening conduct, it only prohibits protected speech. We disagree. The plain language of the statute indicates that it regulates speech and the conduct of "passing a leaflet or handbill," and "displaying a sign." Petitioners also contend that because their speech is directed to everyone, including "innocent" passers-by on the sidewalk who are not entering the health care facility, the statute unduly restricts speech that is intended to be only directed towards passers-by. Again, we disagree.

In rather simple but straight-forward language, the statute prohibits individuals from "knowingly approaching" a person within eight feet without that person's consent.

> "We hold that section 18-9-122(3) is a reasonable restriction on the time, place, and manner of petitioners' speech and, therefore, is valid under the First Amendment."

Under section 18-9-122(3), a criminal statute, two requirements must be met to constitute a violation: (1) the mens rea [mental state] requirement, "knowingly"; and (2) the actus reus [criminal act] requirement, "approaches." If one of the petitioners is standing still within the fixed buffer zone, and an individual walks toward him or her, the petitioner need not change his or her physical positioning to maintain eight feet of distance and thus avoid violating the statute, even if the approaching individual comes within less than eight feet of the petitioner. In other words, so long as the petitioner remains still, he or she cannot commit the actus reus of approaching, even though he or she may well have the requisite mens rea of "knowingly." Thus, in any scenario, petitioners are free to attempt to speak with whomever they wish and they will not violate the statute, so long as the mens rea and actus reus do not coincide. Therefore, any risk of an inadvertent violation involving an "innocent" passer-by is, at most, de minimus [slight].

> *"The fact that the statute may apply to persons entering health care facilities beyond those providing abortion counseling does not render the statute overly restrictive of speech."*

Access to Health Care

Admittedly, under the statute, petitioners may not "knowingly approach" an individual within eight feet unless the petitioner has obtained the individual's consent. What renders this statute less restrictive than both the injunction in *Schenck* and the ordinance in *Sabelko* is that under section 18-9-122(3), there is no duty to withdraw placed upon petitioners even within the eight-foot limited floating buffer zone. Thus, an inadvertent violation caused by a third party is not a legitimate threat here, as all parties conceded at oral arguments. Petitioners also contend that the statute is not narrow enough because it applies to all health care facilities in Colorado. The fact that the statute may apply to persons entering health care facilities beyond those providing abortion counseling does not render the statute overly restrictive of speech. Rather, simply and purposefully, that fact renders the statute comprehensive. Indeed, the applicability of the statute to situations other than anti-abortion protesting is one reason we conclude that the statute is content-neutral. And we decline any invitation on this record to conclude that a facet of a statute that renders it content-neutral necessarily renders it overly broad.

Second, we also hold that the statute furthers a significant government interest. After open public hearings that provide support for its public policy action we review today, the General Assembly declared in section 18-9-122(1) that "access to health care facilities for the purpose of obtaining medical counseling and treatment is imperative for the citizens of this state." Indeed, the statute was enacted, in part, through the General Assembly's police power, and by a General Assembly that was concerned with the safety of individuals seeking wide-ranging health care services, not merely abortion counseling and procedures. Clearly, a fair reading of the legislative record reflects a legislative response to conduct that subjected citizens in Colorado to harassing, confrontational, and violent conduct. We conclude that this express purpose furthers a significant government interest. . . . Moreover, we note that it has long been acknowledged that government "may properly assert important interests in safeguarding health."

Available Channels of Communication

Finally, turning to the last requirement under *Ward,* that ample alternative channels of communication be left open, we similarly conclude that section 18-9-122(3) passes muster. Section 18-9-122(3) does not prohibit verbal communication, as petitioners contend. While the authority to regulate in some instances may include the power to deny, here petitioners' argument is not persuasive. Petitioners, indeed, everyone, are still able to protest, counsel, shout, implore, dissuade, persuade, educate, inform, and distribute literature regarding abortion. They just cannot knowingly approach within eight feet of an individual who is within 100 feet of a health care facility entrance without that individual's consent. As articulated so well by the Supreme Court in *Ward,* "[t]hat [section 18-9-122(3)] may reduce to some degree the potential audience for [petitioners'] speech is of no consequence, for there has been no showing that the remaining avenues of communication are inadequate." In fact, although leafleting is deterred under the statute, petitioners have failed to offer any credible evidence that normal conversation or the communication of their message through demonstrative devices, such as placards and photographs, limits communication of their message. Moreover, because petitioners may knowingly approach up to eight feet of any person, in the parking lot, on the sidewalk, and even at the health care facility door, under the statute at issue here, we fail to see how petitioners' audience is diminished at all. On its face, there is nothing that prohibits protesters from being seen and heard by those accessing health care facilities as well as passers-by.

It is important to emphasize that in [*Schenck v. Pro-Choice Network*, a 1997 ruling] the Supreme Court did not strike down all "floating" buffer zones per se, as the petitioners essentially contend. In striking down the floating buffer zones created by the injunction in *Schenck,* the Court recognized that "there may well be other ways to both effect . . . separation and yet provide certainty (so that speech protected by the injunction's terms is not burdened). . . ." In fact, it was the uncertainty of how to comply with the injunction about which the Supreme Court appeared most concerned. The Court stated that because the protester would have to move with the individual, and because the clinic sidewalks were only seventeen feet wide, "it would be quite difficult for a protester who wishes to engage in peaceful expressive activities to know how to remain in compliance with the injunction. This lack of certainty leads to a

> *"'The right to be let alone,' is consistent with the well-accepted notion that '[t]he First Amendment does not guarantee the right to communicate one's views.'"*

substantial risk that much more speech will be burdened than the injunction by its terms prohibits."

Here, in contrast, the statute is so narrowly drawn that these concerns are alleviated. First, protesters must only maintain a distance of eight feet, not fifteen, which allows for normal conversational tones. Second, where in *Schenck* a protester could have easily violated the injunction merely by standing still if, for example, an individual approached a protester, then that protester would violate the injunction. Here, in contrast, the mens rea "knowingly" requirement ensures that scenario will not be possible. Even if a protester is approached by an individual, the protester will only violate the statute if, along with the several other requirements of the statute, he or she "knowingly approaches" the individual for the purpose of passing a leaflet or engaging in oral protest. The inadvertent violation, or at least the possibility of such a violation, is substantially avoided by the plain terms of the statute. In *Schenck,* in order to avoid violating the injunction, the protesters were obligated to maintain sufficient separation of fifteen feet at all times. There, the movement of a third party could place the protesters in the position of having violated the injunction. Here, to the contrary, petitioners may actually stand still and though individuals may approach within eight feet of petitioners, the requisite actus reus of "approach[ing]" is not met. Thus, we do not believe that, even under the *Schenck* test, section 18-9-122(3) burdens more speech than is necessary.

In sum, we hold that section 18-9-122(3) represents a fair legislative balancing of the "right to protest or counsel against certain medical procedures" while protecting "a person's right to obtain medical counseling and treatment." In addition, we find the General Assembly's statutory response a fair accommodation of two fundamental rights. We also conclude that "the right to be let alone," is consistent with the well-accepted notion that "[t]he First Amendment does not guarantee the right to communicate one's views . . . in any manner that may be desired." Heffron, 452 U.S. at 647 (emphasis added).

Thus, we hold that section 18-9-122(3) is a valid time, place and manner restriction, a permissible legislative response designed to assure safety and order for citizens entering and leaving Colorado health care facilities. It is content-neutral, is narrowly tailored to serve a significant governmental interest, and leaves open ample alternative channels of communication. Accordingly, we affirm the judgment of the court of appeals.

Freedom of Expression Should Be Protected

by American Civil Liberties Union

About the author: *The American Civil Liberties Union is a national organization that opposes regulation of all forms of speech.*

Freedom of speech, of the press, of association, of assembly and petition—this set of guarantees, protected by the First Amendment, comprises what we refer to as freedom of expression. The Supreme Court has written that this freedom is "the matrix, the indispensable condition of nearly every other form of freedom." Without it, other fundamental rights, like the right to vote, would wither and die.

Protecting Free Speech

But in spite of its "preferred position" in our constitutional hierarchy, the nation's commitment to freedom of expression has been tested over and over again. Especially during times of national stress, like war abroad or social upheaval at home, people exercising their First Amendment rights have been censored, fined, even jailed. Those with unpopular political ideas have always borne the brunt of government repression. It was during WWI—hardly ancient history—that a person could be jailed just for giving out anti-war leaflets. Out of those early cases, modern First Amendment law evolved. Many struggles and many cases later, ours is the most speech-protective country in the world.

The path to freedom was long and arduous. It took nearly 200 years to establish firm constitutional limits on the government's power to punish "seditious" and "subversive" speech. Many people suffered along the way, such as labor leader Eugene V. Debs, who was sentenced to 10 years in prison under the Espionage Act just for telling a rally of peaceful workers to realize they were "fit for something better than slavery and cannon fodder." Or Sidney Street, jailed in 1969 for burning an American flag on a Harlem street corner to protest the shooting of civil rights figure James Meredith.

Free speech rights still need constant, vigilant protection. New questions arise

Excerpted from the American Civil Liberties Union, "Freedom of Expression," an online article from www.aclu.org/library/pbp10.html, 1997. Reprinted with permission from the American Civil Liberties Union.

and old ones return. Should flag burning be a crime? What about government or private censorship of works of art that touch on sensitive issues like religion or sexuality? Should the Internet be subject to any form of government control? What about punishing college students who espouse racist or sexist opinions? In answering these questions, the history and the core values of the First Amendment should be our guide.

The Supreme Court and the First Amendment

During our nation's early era, the courts were almost universally hostile to political minorities' First Amendment rights; free speech issues did not even reach the Supreme Court until 1919 when, in *Schenck v. U.S.*, the Court unanimously upheld the conviction of a Socialist Party member for mailing anti-anti-war leaflets to draft-age men. A turning point occurred a few months later in *Abrams v. U.S.* Although the defendant's conviction under the Espionage Act for distributing anti-war leaflets was upheld, two dissenting opinions formed the cornerstone of our modern First Amendment law. Justices Oliver Wendell Holmes and Louis D. Brandeis argued speech could *only*

> *"The nation's commitment to freedom of expression has been tested over and over again."*

be punished *if* it presented "a clear and present danger" of imminent harm. Mere political advocacy, they said, was protected by the First Amendment. Eventually, these justices were able to convince a majority of the Court to adopt the "clear and present danger test."

From then on, the right to freedom of expression grew more secure—until the 1950s and McCarthyism. The Supreme Court fell prey to the witchhunt mentality of that period, seriously weakening the "clear and present danger" test by holding that speakers could be punished if they advocated overthrowing the government—even if the danger of such an occurrence were both slight and remote. As a result, many political activists were prosecuted and jailed simply for advocating communist revolution. Loyalty oath requirements for government employees were upheld; thousands of Americans lost their jobs on the basis of flimsy evidence supplied by secret witnesses.

Finally, in 1969, in *Brandenberg v. Ohio*, the Supreme Court struck down the conviction of a Ku Klux Klan member, and established a new standard: Speech can be suppressed only if it is intended, *and likely to produce*, "imminent lawless action." Otherwise, even speech that advocates violence is protected. The *Brandenberg* standard prevails today.

Protected Speech and Hate Speech

First Amendment protection is not limited to "pure speech"—books, newspapers, leaflets, and rallies. It also protects "symbolic speech"—nonverbal expression whose purpose is to communicate ideas. In its 1969 decision in *Tinker v.*

Des Moines, the Court recognized the right of public school students to wear black armbands in protest of the Vietnam War. In 1989 (*Texas v. Johnson*) and again in 1990 (*U.S. v. Eichman*), the Court struck down government bans on "flag desecration." Other examples of protected symbolic speech include works of art, T-shirt slogans, political buttons, music lyrics and theatrical performances.

> *"If we do not come to the defense of the free speech rights of the most unpopular among us, . . . then no one's liberty will be secure."*

Government can limit some protected speech by imposing "time, place and manner" restrictions. This is most commonly done by requiring permits for meetings, rallies and demonstrations. But a permit cannot be unreasonably withheld, nor can it be denied based on content of the speech. That would be what is called viewpoint discrimination—and *that* is unconstitutional.

When a protest crosses the line from speech to action, the government can intervene more aggressively. Political protesters have the right to picket, to distribute literature, to chant and to engage passersby in debate. But they do not have the right to block building entrances or to physically harass people.

The ACLU has often been at the center of controversy for defending the free speech rights of groups that spew hate, such as the Ku Klux Klan and the Nazis. But if only popular ideas were protected, we wouldn't need a First Amendment. History teaches that the first target of government repression is never the last. If we do not come to the defense of the free speech rights of the most unpopular among us, even if their views are antithetical to the very freedom the First Amendment stands for, then no one's liberty will be secure. In that sense, all First Amendment rights are "indivisible."

Censoring so-called hate speech also runs counter to the long-term interests of the most frequent victims of hate: racial, ethnic, religious and sexual minorities. We should not give the government the power to decide which opinions are hateful, for history has taught us that government is more apt to use this power to prosecute minorities than to protect them. As one federal judge has put it, tolerating hateful speech is "the best protection we have against any Nazi-type regime in this country."

At the same time, freedom of speech does not prevent punishing conduct that intimidates, harasses, or threatens another person, even if words are used. Threatening phone calls, for example, are not constitutionally protected.

Speech and National Security

The Supreme Court has recognized the government's interest in keeping some information secret, such as wartime troop deployments. But the Court has never actually upheld an injunction against speech on national security grounds. Two lessons can be learned from this historical fact. First, the amount of speech that can be curtailed in the interest of national security is very limited. And second, the government has historically overused the concept of "national security" to shield itself from criticism, and to discourage public discussion of controversial policies or decisions.

In 1971, the publication of the "Pentagon Papers" by the *New York Times* brought the conflicting claims of free speech and national security to a head. The Pentagon Papers, a voluminous secret history and analysis of the country's involvement in Vietnam, was leaked to the press. When the *Times* ignored the government's demand that it cease publication, the stage was set for a Supreme Court decision. In the landmark *U.S. v. New York Times* case, the Court ruled that the government could not, through "prior restraint," block publication of any material unless it could prove that it would "surely" result in "direct, imme-diate, and irreparable" harm to the nation. This the government failed to prove, and the public was given access to vital information about an issue of enormous importance.

The public's First Amendment "right to know" is essential to its ability to fully participate in democratic decision-making. As the Pentagon Papers case demonstrates, the government's claims of "national security" must always be closely scrutinized to make sure they are valid.

Exceptions to the First Amendment

The Supreme Court has recognized several limited exceptions to First Amendment protection.

• In *Chaplinsky v. New Hampshire* (1942), the Court held that so-called "fighting words . . . which by their very utterance inflict injury or tend to incite an immediate breach of the peace," are not protected. This decision was based on the fact that fighting words are of "slight social value as a step to truth."

• In *New York Times Co. v. Sullivan* (1964), the Court held that defamatory falsehoods about public officials can be punished—*only* if the offended official can prove the falsehoods were published with "actual malice," i.e.: "knowledge that the statement was false or with reckless disregard of whether it was false or not." Other kinds of "libelous statements" are also punishable.

> *"The obscenity exception to the First Amendment is highly subjective and practically invites government abuse."*

• Legally "obscene" material has historically been excluded from First Amendment protection. Unfortu-nately, the relatively narrow obscen-ity exception, described below, has been abused by government authori-ties and private pressure groups. Sexual expression in art and entertainment is, and has historically been, the most frequent target of censorship crusades, from James Joyce's classic *Ulysses* to the photographs of Robert Mapplethorpe.

In the 1973 *Miller v. California* decision, the Court established three conditions that must be present if a work is to be deemed "legally obscene." It must 1) appeal to the average person's prurient (shameful, morbid) interest in sex; 2) depict sexual conduct in a "patently offensive way" as defined by community standards; and 3) taken as a whole, lack serious literary, artistic, political or scientific value. Attempts to apply the "Miller test" have demonstrated the impossibility of formulating a precise definition of obscenity. Justice Potter Stewart once delivered a famous one-liner on the subject: "I know it when I see it." But the fact is, the obscenity exception to the First Amendment is highly subjective and practically invites government abuse.

The ACLU's Role in Protecting Free Speech

The American Civil Liberties Union has been involved in virtually all of the landmark First Amendment cases to reach the U.S. Supreme Court, and remains absolutely committed to the preservation of each and every individual's freedom of expression. During the 1980s, we defended the right of artists and entertainers to perform and produce works of art free of government and private censorship. During the 1990s, the organization fought to protect free speech in cyberspace when state and federal government attempted to impose content-based regulations on the Internet. In addition, the ACLU offers several books on the subject of freedom of expression.

Hate Speech Should Not Be Censored

by Charles Levendosky

About the author: *Charles Levendosky is the editorial page director of the* Star-Tribune *in Casper, Wyoming.*

Sex and lurking sexual predators aren't the only worries people have about the Internet. Web sites that blaze with hate and bigotry have also come under fire recently. And unfortunately, there are those who would hack a hunk out of the First Amendment in order to ban such sites.

Hate Speech on the World Wide Web

Hate speech on the Internet has grown rapidly—through Web sites, e-mail, bulletin boards and chat rooms—according to a study published by the Anti-Defamation League last year. The ADL monitors the Internet looking for anti-Semitic speech propagated by neo-Nazi, white supremacist groups. In the study, "High-Tech Hate: Extremist Use of the Internet," the ADL notes that hate Web sites more than doubled in one year, from 1996 to 1997.

Hate speech can be loosely defined as speech that reviles or ridicules a person or group of people based upon their race, creed, sexual orientation, religion, handicap, economic condition or national origin,

A number of universities, more sensitive to people's feelings than the significance of the First Amendment, have written speech regulations to punish students who post hate messages on the World Wide Web. Some universities have put blocking technology on their computers that have Internet access—to filter out Web sites that advocate racism, anti-Semitism, white supremacy, homophobia, Holocaust denial, sexual superiority, anti-government vigilante justice, and other forms of prejudice and bigotry.

There are those who push for a rating system for every Web page, with stiff fines for those who didn't rate their sites or rated them wrongly.

Presumably an Aryan Nations or Ku Klux Klan site would have to rate itself (or be rated by others) so that children could not gain access when the appropri-

Reprinted from Charles Levendosky, "One Man's Hate Speech, Another's Political Speech," *Liberal Opinion Week*, August 17, 1998. Reprinted with permission from the author.

ate filtering program is installed to read the ratings and block some categories.

The Southern Poverty Law Center in Montgomery, Ala., labelled the Nation of Islam as a hate group in a recent report.

The company that makes the software filter called Cyber Patrol made a decision months ago to block out the American Family Association's Web site because it contains prejudicial statements against homosexuality.

The right-wing American Family Association, ironically, has pushed parents, schools and libraries to use Internet filters like Cyber Patrol.

A number of academics argue that hate speech should not be protected by the First Amendment. Fortunately, their arguments have not been persuasive against our long and honored tradition of free speech.

Hate Speech Is Often Political

While we may despise the comments made on some of these hate-filled Web sites, it is difficult to argue they are not espousing a political position. Often one man's hate speech is another man's political statement. And political commentary has—and should have—the highest First Amendment protection.

As the U.S. Supreme Court noted in finding the Communications Decency Act unconstitutional last year, anyone with access to the Internet can be a pamphleteer sending e-mail messages to thousands of recipients with one click of a button, or posting Web sites that are eventually seen by hundreds of thousands. It is the most democratic communication media yet devised.

The leading edge of any social or political movement cuts a path to recognition by using radical, sometimes outrageous rhetoric. The rhetoric is there to define or redefine the landscape in terms that suit that particular movement. It is there to shake up the prevailing state of affairs. This has been true in this nation from the time of our own revolution to gain independence from Great Britain to the present.

Certainly, the British Crown could have considered the Declaration of Independence a form of hate speech.

The Industrial Workers of the World, the labor movement, the socialist movement, anti-war movements, the Black Power movement, poverty marches, veteran's marches, the temperance crusade, women's liberation movement, the anti-abortion movement—all used inflammatory rhetoric like a blowtorch to burn a hole in the status quo. To demand that people take sides. And see the world differently.

If hate speech were prohibited, socio-political movements could be crushed before they even started.

Reasons for Hate Speech

The current cliche about "civility" in debate may be fine when we all agree to basic premises and we're all well fed and treated equally. We can afford to be polite to one another and chummy. But civility does not serve the downtrodden, the forgotten, the invisible, the persecuted, the hungry and homeless. Civility in pursuit of justice plays to the power structure's selective deafness. To be effective, the voice must be raised, the tone sharpened, the language at a pitch that slices the air.

Americans know this at heart—we were born in a revolution.

> *"Often one man's hate speech is another man's political statement. And political commentary has—and should have—the highest First Amendment protection."*

Hate speech is not the cause of bigotry, but arises out of it and a sense of political and social powerlessness. Allowing those who feel powerless to speak—no matter how vehement the language—salves the speaker. Venting frustration, anger and hurt is an important use of language. It may actually short circuit an inclination for physical violence.

The black playwright Imamu Amiri Baraka (LeRoi Jones) had one of his characters in "Dutchman," his 1960s play about a black rebellion, say that for every poem he wrote, there was one less white man he killed.

Suppressing Speech Can Have Ill Effects

Suppressing speech, even hateful speech and perhaps especially hateful speech, would inevitably lead to violence.

We don't protect the civil rights of those who are targets of hateful speech by suppressing the speech of hate mongers. For eventually, inexorably, such suppression turns and bites those it is supposed to protect.

Speech laws that have been adopted to protect racial minorities are actually used to persecute the very people they were created to protect.

This has been true in Great Britain and in Canada—just as it has been true at universities in the United States.

When the University of Michigan put its speech code against racist speech into effect and before the code was struck down in 1989 as unconstitutional, 20 students were charged with violations. Ironically only one was punished, a black student for using the term "white trash."

The power structure interprets and enforces the law. Where white males dominate, white males are less likely to be prosecuted under such laws—cynical but true.

Suppressing hate speech is more dangerous than allowing it to exist.

Like it or not, hate speech has a role to play in a nation dedicated to vigorous debate about public issues.

Flag Desecration Should Not Be Banned

by People for the American Way

About the author: *People for the American Way is an organization that fights for constitutional freedoms, justice, and civil rights.*

If passed and ratified, a constitutional amendment to ban flag desecration would be the first in our nation's history to restrict the core freedoms in our Bill of Rights.

Passage and ratification of the flag desecration amendment would cause serious and irrevocable damage to the architecture of the Constitution and the fundamental freedoms guaranteed by the Bill of Rights, the very freedoms that separate the United States from totalitarian regimes and that make the United States a beacon of liberty to the world.

The Effects of a Flag Amendment

As discussed below, while the long-term consequences of such an unprecedented change to our fundamental charter cannot be fully known now, which is reason enough for not charting such a dangerous and unnecessary course,

THE FLAG AMENDMENT WOULD:

1. embolden those who are currently seeking to pass religious and other amendments to the Bill of Rights and make such further amendments to our core principles more likely;

2. profoundly alter First Amendment law and the freedoms we enjoy in areas entirely outside the flag desecration debate;

3. increase precipitously the number, divisiveness, and resulting harm of acts of civil disobedience and protest involving flag desecration.

A Dangerous Precedent

If ratified, the flag amendment will establish a dangerous precedent that will make it easier for others to enact restrictive amendments to the Bill of Rights in the future. Furthermore, the amendment's success would encourage those who wish to use similar amendments as cynical, political tools. [As of January 2000, no such amendment had been approved by the Senate or ratified by thirty-eight states.]

Those who support the amendment argue that the flag is a special case, and ratification of the flag amendment would not lead to other such amendments. However, this view is shortsighted and ignores the significant precedential effect that the amendment's presence in the Constitution would have. Already, many constitutional amendments are proposed each year—106 constitutional amendments were introduced in the House and Senate during the 105th Congress. Of those, 24 would have altered the Bill of Rights. Some, such as the Religious Freedom Amendment, command significant support. Establishing the principle that the First Amendment can be restricted by constitutional amendment would give supporters of other restrictive amendments ammunition and momentum and weaken public respect and support for safeguarding the enduring principles in our Bill of Rights.

Given the unfortunate modern reality of "wedge issue" politics, this certainly will not be the last time that legislators who care deeply about the Bill of Rights will be forced to choose between their respect for the enduring principles of the Constitution and support for a poll-tested constitutional amendment without regard to the need or consequences of such an amendment. Indeed, the Religious Freedom Amendment provides a good example of the type of cynical and divisive tactic that the flag amendment would only encourage: *some supporters of the so-called "Religious Freedom" Amendment wrongly mislabel their opponents as "against religion" much as opponents of the flag amendment are sometimes wrongly painted as "against the flag or country" when nothing could be further from the truth.* Ratification of the flag amendment will only embolden and strengthen the hand of those pushing other equally divisive amendments that will force legislators of good will to pay a perceived and perhaps increasing political price for safeguarding our constitutional principles for future generations.

The Flag Amendment Would Weaken Other First Amendment Protections

Because it would reflect the most recent statement of Congress on First Amendment matters, ratification of a flag desecration amendment could profoundly undermine the fundamental protections in the First Amendment for debate and dissent, particularly for unpopular or controversial expression at any given moment in history. Specifically, it would undermine what the Supreme Court has described as "the bedrock principle underlying the First Amendment . . . that the Government may not prohibit the expression of an idea simply because society finds the idea itself offensive and disagreeable." Moreover, the flag desecration amendment could seriously threaten the well-accepted protections provided by the First Amendment for non-verbal political and cultural expression, as in political cartoons, posters, paintings and other artwork.

Supporters of the amendment claim that it would carve out an isolated exception to the First Amendment's core principles and that flag desecration can be separated from other forms of expression. This claim is wrong and shortsighted. As a matter of accepted legal analysis, in future cases affecting First Amendment rights outside the flag context, legal advocates and courts will look to the flag amendment as a more recent reflection of Congress's view of First Amendment principles, and to the broader proposition for which the amendment would stand: i.e., that political expression can be limited based on its content and viewpoint, and that the protection of a national symbol is a compelling reason to do so.

> *"Ratification of a flag desecration amendment could profoundly undermine the fundamental protections in the First Amendment for debate and dissent."*

Our own history provides frightening examples of harmful laws passed in the name of protecting national symbols and national unity that only were overturned because of the strength of our First Amendment principles: the Alien and Sedition Act of 1798, loyalty oaths, and compulsory flag salute laws. The "central meaning" of the First Amendment has protected our nation against these temporary majoritarian abuses that would have undermined our fundamental freedoms of expression, association, and criticism of governmental policies and officials. It is precisely with these types of laws, justified during difficult historical situations as necessary to preserve national unity or patriotism, that a proposed flag "desecration" amendment could most easily be used to undermine the bedrock First Amendment principles which have safeguarded our liberties against attempted usurpations for over 200 years.

An Ironic Increase in Flag Desecrations

History has shown that flag desecration, while overall exceedingly rare, is typically at its peak when Congress acts to outlaw flag desecration, either as a result of attention seekers or civil disobedience. The latest such peak happened in 1989, when many people burned flags to protest the passage of the Flag Protection Act (FPA) after the *Johnson v. Texas* case. The FPA was soon overturned by the Supreme Court in the *Eichman* decision, and according to the Congressional Research Service there were only a handful of flag burnings between 1990 and 1995—at which time Congress again moved to ban flag desecration.

According to Professor Robert Justin Goldstein of Oakland University, who has written several books on the flag desecration controversy, there were fewer than 45 reported incidents of flag burning in the over 200 years between 1777 when the flag was adopted, and 1989, and about half of these occurred during the Vietnam War era. *With Congressional efforts to outlaw flag desecration and the corresponding media attention, there have been more than twice as many flag burnings since 1989 than in the entire rest of the nation's history.*

Given this history, the reaction to the passage of a constitutional amendment

giving Congress the power to ban flag desecration is likely to be even more se-
vere and prolonged. Flag burnings will occur in protest, just as they did in
1989, but this time they would probably be more numerous and the rise in activity will be more prolonged. Incidents of flag burnings would likely be ele-
vated in number throughout the ratification process, after passage of the first
law under the amendment, and during the inevitable and drawn-out litigation
over the interpretation of the first flag statute and any subsequent statutes Congress might decide to enact.

*Thus, ironically, passage of a flag amendment will dramatically increase,
rather than decrease, incidents of flag desecration.* The result will only be to
increase the pain and divisiveness caused by such incidents and perhaps to re-
open old Vietnam War–era wounds that the nation has largely healed. This certainly is no way to unite and protect our country, its cherished symbols, or the
very freedoms for which the flag stands.

Anti-Abortion Protests Should Not Be Censored

by Edward McGlynn Gaffney Jr.

About the author: *Edward McGlynn Gaffney Jr. is a professor of law at Valparasio University in Indiana.*

Since 1993 there have been seven murders and fourteen attempted murders of abortion-clinic personnel, as well as more than two hundred clinic bombings and arsons. In this atmosphere one can readily understand that those who work in abortion clinics feel physically endangered. But by whom? By protesters who speak out against what happens in the clinics? Where should the line be drawn between protesters' free-speech rights and what the law calls "true threats" or extortion? Does a website that included names and addresses of abortion clinics and doctors and that offers cash rewards for the prevention of abortions amount to threatening and provocative speech beyond the protection of the First Amendment?

Lawsuits Against Anti-Abortion Protesters

A recent case in Portland, Oregon, imposed civil liability on anti-abortion protesters for activity that abortion providers found threatening. A local chapter of Planned Parenthood and individual physicians who provide abortions in Planned Parenthood clinics brought their suit under both the Freedom of Access to Clinic Entrances Act (1994), which makes it illegal to use "force or threat of force" against abortion clients or providers, and the Racketeer Influenced and Corrupt Organizations (RICO) law. The primary focus of the suit was a website called the "Nuremberg Files" (found on the Web at christiangallery.com/atrocity), operated by the principal defendants, the American Coalition of Life Activists (ACLA). The website featured the names and addresses of abortion clinics and doctors, and offered cash rewards for the prevention of abortions. Deciding that ACLA had gone beyond constitutionally protected political speech by threatening abortion providers, the jury ordered the coalition to pay $107 million in damages.

In recent times, the Supreme Court has set a high standard of protection for political protest. In *Madsen v. Women's Health Center* (1994), the Court disallowed an injunction preventing abortion opponents from approaching persons seeking services at an abortion clinic unless there was "evidence that the protesters' speech is independently proscribable (that is, 'fighting words' or threats), or is so infused with violence as to be indistinguishable from a threat of physical harm." The Court added in *Schenck v. Pro-Choice Network* (1997) that there is no legitimate government interest in protecting the "right of the people approaching and entering [clinics] to be left alone" on the public streets, traditionally open to all sorts of communications. Still, the question of what constitutes a threat remains slippery. Some lower courts have diluted the idea of a threat to mean virtually any words that do not support the tentative decision of a woman to have an abortion.

Court Reactions to Political Speech

Anti-abortion protest is political speech, normally to be accorded broad protection. Think of tough labor organizers urging scabs not to cross a picket line. In a host of labor law decisions, the Court has protected some pretty rough talk as long as there was no physical violence. Sometimes the Court has even understood that name-calling can lead to blows, and has looked the other way to preserve what Justice William Brennan described as "the central meaning of the First Amendment . . . the 'profound national commitment' that 'debate on public issues should be uninhibited, robust, and wide open.'"

> *"Anti-abortion protest is political speech, normally to be accorded broad protection."*

For example, the Court dealt sensibly with a famous economic boycott called by a Mississippi chapter of the National Association for the Advancement of Colored People (NAACP) from 1966 to 1973 to protest the failure of local officials to desegregate public schools, hire black police officers, or include blacks on juries. Charles Evers, the NAACP field secretary, made a number of fiery speeches, warning "Uncle Toms" who broke the boycott that they would "have their necks broken by their own people." "Enforcers" stood guard at the doors of boycotted businesses to take down the names of blacks frequenting them. The names were published in a local black newspaper and read aloud at NAACP meetings. For most boycott violators, punishment stopped at being called demeaning names, but sometimes physical coercion followed.

In *NAACP v. Claiborne Hardware* (1977), the Court reversed the huge damage award that the stores had won against the civil rights organization in the state court. Evidently the NAACP's physical intimidation of the boycott breakers was not significant enough to forfeit the group's free speech rights or force them to pay disproportionate financial damages. The Court was willing to countenance clearly threatening language in order to protect the NAACP's vital role in promoting civil rights activity.

Not True Threats

It is difficult to extend constitutional protection to the message of the NAACP and withhold it from the message espoused by abortion protesters. Some simply pray silently in front of a clinic. Others express their views by holding a placard either with a slogan like "An abortion stops a beating heart," or with a disturbing photograph. But we shouldn't imagine that on an issue as deeply divisive as abortion those who take their protest to the streets—on either side of the divide—will always be polite. Or logical. ACLA publishes *A Time to Kill,* a short book in which one of the named defendants, Michael Bray, argues that the use of force is legitimate to protect the lives lost in abortion facilities, a position abhorrent to those of us committed to a consistent ethic of life.

Still, the courts will get into a hopeless morass and our public life will be enfeebled unless speech of all sorts is protected, except—as the Court ruled in *Brandenberg v. Ohio* (1968)—where it is actually likely to result in imminent danger of violence. Planned Parenthood does its cause no service by complaining about the distribution of bumper stickers urging the execution of abortionists as murderers, or about "Wanted" posters that do not specifically identify doctors or clinics by name. However disturbing these forms of communication might be, they do not constitute true threats and should be protected by the First Amendment.

More worrisome is Planned Parenthood's use of the federal RICO statute, designed as a weapon against organized crime, to silence and financially bankrupt their political adversaries. As the feminist author Wendy Kaminer has written, the RICO statute "was not supposed to brand ideologically motivated activists as racketeers or extortionists." The most dubious legal claim advanced by Planned Parenthood is that ACLA violated RICO by maintaining "The Nuremberg Files." As its title suggests, the website expects that abortion providers "will be charged in perfectly legal courts once the tide of this nation's opinion turns against the wanton slaughter of God's children." Recording information about abortion providers for the purpose of bringing them to justice in a procedurally fair manner seems clearly within the realm of protected speech. ACLA's website also published the names and addresses of 225 doctors who perform abortions. The names of those classified as "working" were printed in black font, those "wounded" ap-

> *"Planned Parenthood does its cause no service by complaining about the distribution of bumper stickers urging the execution of abortionists as murderers."*

peared in gray, and fatalities had a strikethrough across their name. Planned Parenthood and their doctors testified that they feel threatened by this, as though ACLA had identified targets on a hit list. A spokesman for ACLA defended the "fatality" notice as merely reportorial. Currently, the website no longer publishes a list of names, but still seeks help in gathering evidence identifying abortion providers and "judges and politicians who pass or uphold laws authorizing [abortions] or oppressing prolife activists."

Now that the court has allowed a huge penalty (RICO permits courts to triple damage awards) against the ACLA website on the ground that it "threatens" life, the appellate court will have to decide whether there was enough of a serious threat to extinguish the protection of the First Amendment. ACLA argues that their statements were intended to protect, not to threaten, life. The trial judge determined that a speaker's intent is irrelevant, instructing the jury under the current standard in the Ninth Circuit that a threat is determined "objectively" by focusing on what a reasonable and informed listener would make of the words. But there are different standards in various circuits. For instance, the Second Circuit in New York requires jurors to take a speaker's intent into account, ruling that free-speech protection can only be revoked if "the threat on its face and in the circumstances in which it is made is so unequivocal, unconditional, immediate, and specific as to the person threatened, as to convey a gravity of purpose and imminent prospect of execution." Unless the Ninth Circuit modifies its view, this case may be headed for the Supreme Court to resolve the apparent conflict between the circuits. The Court has not favored congressional efforts to police the Internet, striking down the Communications Decency Act in *Reno v. ACLU* (1997). But if the high court takes this case, the radical rhetoric of the anti-abortionists may further complicate things. In the past the website has included among the "abortionists' shysters" six justices: Sandra Day O'Connor, David Souter, Anthony Kennedy, John Paul Stevens, Ruth Bader Ginsburg, and—most curiously—Byron White (the retired justice who denounced Roe in a stinging dissent as an "exercise in raw judicial power"). Time will tell whether life-tenured justices also feel threatened by such talk.

Chapter 2

Does Censorship Occur in the Educational System?

Chapter Preface

Mark Twain's *The Adventures of Huckleberry Finn* is one of the most-read and most-censored books. Since its publication in 1885, the story of the boy Huck and the runaway slave Jim has been targeted for censorship. The Concord Public Library in Massachusetts banned the book in spring 1885, charging that the dialect used by the narrator Huck was "rough, coarse and inelegant." The *New York Herald* explained that the Concord Library Committee "have unanimously reached the conclusion that *Huckleberry Finn* is not the sort of reading matter for . . . knowledge seekers." In 1902 and 1905, the book was banned from the public libraries in Denver and Brooklyn, respectively.

By the middle of the twentieth century, many people remained concerned about the language used in *Huckleberry Finn*, although for different reasons than those proposed by the Concord library. With the rise of the civil rights movement in the 1950s, efforts to ban or censure *Huckleberry Finn* were predicated on the belief held by many people that the book was racist, due to the depiction of Jim—whom many viewed as a caricature too easily tricked by Huck and Tom Sawyer—and the repeated use of the word "nigger." In 1957, the National Association for the Advancement of Colored People labeled the book "racially offensive" and New York City removed *Huckleberry Finn* from its list of approved books for junior and senior high schools.

Over the past decade, *Huckleberry Finn* has repeatedly been at or near the top of the American Library Association's list of most-banned books. Responding to parents' complaints, schools in Connecticut, Washington, D.C., and elsewhere have removed the book from their reading lists. In 1997, Kathy Monteiro argued that the book worsened racial tensions at the Arizona high school her daughter attended and went to court to have the book removed from the school's reading list. The following year, the Ninth Circuit Court of Appeals ruled against banning books based on their content. These efforts to ban *Huckleberry Finn* have been criticized by opponents of censorship, who feel that the book is not racist and can in fact lead to positive discussion about race relations. Many Twain scholars have argued that Twain was racially progressive for his time and created in Jim a moral, honorable character. Jim Zwick, who has published numerous articles about Twain, writes: "Removing the book from school curriculums and libraries . . . [will inhibit] discussion of existing racial divisions instead of addressing them in a positive manner."

The controversy over *The Adventures of Huckleberry Finn* is an example of the debate about whether schools should place restrictions on what their students can learn and discuss. In the following chapter, the authors debate the extent of censorship in the educational system.

Speech Is Censored on College Campuses

by Alan Charles Kors and Harvey A. Silverglate

About the authors: *Alan Charles Kors is a history professor at the University of Pennsylvania in Philadelphia. Harvey A. Silverglate is a lawyer.*

Many in the academy insist that the entire phenomenon labeled "political correctness" is the mythical fabrication of opponents of "progressive" change. They argue that political correctness does not exist as a systematic, coercive, repressive force on American campuses. They claim that critics of universities have questionable motives and offer merely recycled anecdotes, not hard evidence, of abuses of power. For example, the authors of an American Association of University Professors' (AAUP) special committee report, "Statement on the 'Political Correctness' Controversy," insisted, without irony, that claims of "political correctness" were merely smokescreens to hide the true agenda of such critics—a racist and sexist desire to thwart the aspirations of minorities and women in the academic enterprise.

Colleges Are Repressive

Such views seem so very odd to those—students, faculty, and close observers—who dissent from prevailing campus orthodoxies, and who experience the unremitting reality of speech codes (or, more precisely, of the "verbal behavior" provisions of "harassment" policies), of ideological litmus tests, and of sensitivity or diversity "training" that undertakes the involuntary thought reform of free, young minds. It is almost inconceivable that anyone of good faith could live on a college campus unaware of the repression, legal inequality, intrusions into private conscience, and malignant double standards that hold sway there. One charge of verbal harassment casts a pall over everyone's "thought crimes," producing systemic self-censorship, but defenders of the current academic regimes list that merely as "one" instance of (in many of their views, quite justifiable) constraint.

However, when those who deny the power of political correctness think about the McCarthy period [in the 1950s, Senator Joseph McCarthy accused many U.S. officials of being Communists], when repression came from the Right, they understand fully and unambiguously how a climate of repression achieves its results without producing a massive body count (to match the massive spirit count) on every campus. In the Left's history of the McCarthy period, the firing or dismissal of one professor or student, the inquisition into the private beliefs of one individual, let alone the demands for a demonstration of fealty to community standards—in that case, a partisan notion of "Americanism" (as now it is a partisan notion of "multiculturalism")—stand out as intolerable oppressions that coerced people into silence, hypocrisy, betrayal, and the withering or numbing of individual freedom. The claim that McCarthyism was a myth, and

that a small number of anecdotes had been recycled to create the appearance of systematic repression, would be met with incredulous (and justifiable) outrage by the Left.

> *"It is almost inconceivable that anyone of good faith could live on a college campus unaware of the repression . . . that [holds] sway there."*

In fact, in today's assault on liberty on college campuses, there are not a small number of cases, nor a small number of speech codes, nor a small number of apparatuses of repression and thought reform. Number aside, however, it is nonetheless true that a climate of repression succeeds not by statistical frequency, but by sapping the courage, autonomy, and conscience of individuals who otherwise might remember or revive what liberty could be.

Human history teaches that those who wield power rarely see their own abuse of it. This failing pervades the entire ideological, political, cultural, and historical spectrum. It is not an issue of left and right, but of human ethical incapacity. In [Charles Louis] Montesquieu's eighteenth-century classic of social commentary *The Persian Letters*, the traveler Uzbek is exquisitely aware of every injustice that he encounters in the world—except the ruthless injustice of his own vile despotism over his harem and his dependents. There is much of Uzbek in all of us.

Dissent Should Be Respected

Those who exercise power, in any domain, tend to compare their actual power to their ultimate goals, usually concluding from this that they barely have any power at all, and, certainly, that they are not abusing what little they have. Further, most of us sadly develop the capacity to treat the suffering, oppression, or legal inequality of individuals or groups whom we see as obstacles to our own goals or visions—or even with whom we merely feel little affinity—as abstractions or exaggerations without concrete human immediacy. By the same token, most of us experience the suffering, oppression, or legal inequality of individuals or groups with whom we identify, or to whom our own causes are linked, as vivid, intolerable, personal realities. It is precisely to neutralize this grievous tendency of human nature that societies establish formal law, equal justice, and the prohibition of double standards.

Open-minded readers should . . . put themselves with human empathy in the place of those who now dissent sincerely, as is their right, from regnant beliefs and values. Our colleges and universities do not offer the protection of fair rules, equal justice, and standards for all seasons to the generation that finds itself on our campuses. No one who denies such protections to others has any honest claim upon them in the future.

Most students respect disagreement and difference, and they do not bring charges of harassment against those whose opinions or expressions "offend" them. The universities themselves, however, encourage such charges to be brought. At almost every college and university, students deemed members of "historically oppressed groups"—above all, women, blacks, gays, and Hispanics—are informed during orientations that their campuses are teeming with illegal or intolerable violations of their "right" not to be offended. To believe many new-student orientations would be to believe that there was a racial or sexual bigot, to borrow the mocking phrase of McCarthy's critics, "under every bed." At almost every college and university, students are presented with lists of a vast array of places to which they should submit charges of such verbal "harassment," and they are promised "victim support," "confidentiality," and sympathetic understanding when they file such complaints.

> *"Our colleges and universities do not offer the protection of fair rules, equal justice, and standards for all seasons to the generation that finds itself on our campuses."*

What an astonishing expectation (and power) to give to students: the belief that, if they belong to a protected category, they have a right to four years of never being offended. What an extraordinary power to give to administrators and tribunals: the prerogative to punish the free speech and expression of people to whom they choose to assign the stains and guilt of historical oppression, while being free, themselves, to use whatever rhetoric they wish against the bearers of such stains. While the world looks at issues of curriculum and scholarship, above all, to analyze and evaluate American colleges and universities, it is, in fact, the silencing and punishment of belief, expression, and individuality that ought to concern yet more deeply those who care about what universities are and could be. The assault on free expression has proceeded dramatically, largely hidden from public view. Most cases never reach the public, because most individuals accused of "verbal" harassment sadly (but understandably) accept plea bargains that diminish their freedom but spare them Draconian penalties, including expulsion. Even so, the files on prosecutions under speech codes are, alas, overflowing.

Chapter 2

Attacks on Free Speech

Freedom is a fragile and composite thing, and people assail any part of it at their peril. It surprised no civil libertarian that the first victims of Ontario's feminist-inspired antipornography legislation were the writings and bookstores of lesbian feminists. If you tear down laws protecting freedom, they will not be there to protect you. The alternative to the rule of law is the use of force. What people sow, they eventually reap.

Speech codes, with all of their formal clauses, are in fact a parody of the rule of law. This is seen best when these seemingly legalistic codes are subjected to the actual rule of law, which occurs when the speech restrictions of harassment policies at public universities are summoned to the bar of legal scrutiny. Speech, in fact, is freest at public universities because administrators of state universities are aware, at some level, that they are state agencies, bound by the restrictions on state power over individual liberty set out in federal and state constitutions. If a public university violates one's constitutional rights, one can go to court. By contrast, professors and students at private universities are far less likely to take their cases public. They lack recourse to any "appellate" tribunal location capable of commanding an administration to honor freedom. Though more cases are brought against public universities (because of this appellate jurisdiction), their speech codes are certainly not stronger than those of private universities. In their more open record, one sees the nature and mechanisms of the current assault on liberty.

Despite the profound importance, symbolic and substantive, of speech codes, we should not view their presence or absence as the yardstick of freedom. Freedom dies in the heart and will before it dies in the law. Speech codes merely formalize the will to censor and to devalue liberty of thought and speech. Even without invoking codes, universities have found ways to silence or to chill freedom of opinion and expression. Defenders of free speech at colleges and universities become tarred by the sorts of speech they must defend if they wish to defend freedom in general. No one who defends trial by jury over popular justice in a murder trial is called a defender of murder; such a person is seen, by all, as a defender of trial by jury The defender of free speech, however, is forever being told, on American campuses, that he or she is seeking, specifically, to make the campus safe for "racism," "sexism," or "homophobia." That is true if what one means is that the defender of free speech seeks to make the campus safe for the expression of all views, and for the clash of visions, ideas, and passions. At the time of Senator McCarthy, many were intimidated into silence by the question "Why would you want to protect the speech of a Red if you are not a Red?" The issue, then and now, is not the protection of this or that person's rights by our subjective

> *"Speech codes, with all of their formal clauses, are in fact a parody of the rule of law."*

criteria of who deserves freedom, but the protection of freedom itself.

Protection of free speech is not needed for inoffensive, popular speech with which all or most members of a community agree. Such speech is not threatened. Freedom is required precisely for unpopular speech, the toleration of which is one of the marks of a free society. At some point, and in some location, of course, what is popular speech in one place becomes unpopular speech elsewhere. That is why, morally and practically, none of us enjoys more freedom of speech than is accorded the least popular speaker. At a university, of course, no one has an inherent right to be a professor. Universities have ample time, at the moments of hiring, promotion, and tenure, to review a teacher's and a scholar's work, and to decide if it meets their standards. Such power of review should be exercised with tolerant respect for honest differences of opinion—universities depend on that—but it should be exercised. Once in a classroom, however, or conducting research, professors should be free, indeed encouraged, to teach without penalty what they believe to be the truth about their fields of inquiry. Such a system is indeed as messy as human freedom itself. Each of us can name professors whose appointment and subsequent tenure by a university are, for us, objects of wonderment and despair. The lists, however, will not be the same. One's objection to such cases, if one values academic freedom, must be to the act of appointment and tenure (as having been made on inappropriate or inadequately critical academic grounds), and not to the freedom bestowed.

> *"Freedom is required precisely for unpopular speech, the toleration of which is one of the marks of a free society."*

The Double Standards of Speech Codes

The speech-code provisions of harassment policies are merely symptoms of the willful assault on liberty on our campuses: the suppression and punishment of controversial and unpopular ideas; the banning of terms that offend listeners invested with special rights; and the outlawing of discourse that, in the eyes of the defenders of the new orthodoxies, "creates a hostile environment." The essential purpose of a speech code is to repress speech. It may serve other ends, such as making its framers feel moral, powerful, or simply safe from the attacks of those who would criticize them. It also demonstrates, for all to observe, who controls the symbolic environment of a place—a heady feeling for the wielders of power, and a demonstration, of course, that also succeeds in silencing others.

If colleges and universities were beset not by the current "political orthodoxy" but by some other claim for the unequal assignment of protections and rights—"religious orthodoxy" or "patriotic orthodoxy," for example—victims of those calls for repression and double standards would find the evil obvious. Imagine secular, skeptical, or leftist faculty and students confronted by a religious harassment code that prohibited "denigration" of evangelical or Catholic beliefs, or that made the classroom or campus a space where evangelical or Catholic students must be protected against feeling "intimidated," "offended," or, by their own subjective experience, victims of "a hostile environment." Imagine a university of patriotic "loyalty oaths" where leftists were deemed responsible for the tens of millions of victims of communism, and where free minds were prohibited from creating a hostile environment for patriots, or from offending that "minority" of individuals who are descended from Korean War or Vietnam War veterans. Imagine, as well, that for every "case" that became public, there were scores or hundreds of cases in which the "offender" or "victimizer," desperate to preserve a job or gain a degree, accepted a confidential plea bargain that included a semester's or a year's reeducation in "religious sensitivity" or "patriotic sensitivity" seminars run by the university's "Evangelical Center," "Patriotic Center," or "Office of Religious and Patriotic Compliance." Living daily in such a climate—and climates do change—would the same defenders of current codes and repressions call for quantitative studies of the effects of such speech codes on the general academic population?

Speech codes, to the very extent that they are successful, repress by the fear they inspire, not by the number of public cases they produce, and not by the frequency with which a teacher or student risks everything to fight their provisions in a campus trial. Imagine a campus on which being denounced for "irreligious bigotry" or "un-Americanism" carried the same stigma that being denounced for "racism," "sexism," and "homophobia" now carries in the academic world, so that in such hearings or trials, the burden of proof invariably fell upon the "offender." A common sign at prochoice rallies—"Keep your rosaries off our ovaries"— would be prima facie evidence of language used as a weapon to degrade and marginalize, and the common term of abuse—"born-again bigot"—would be compelling evidence of the choice to create a hostile environment for evangelicals. What panegyrics to liberty and free expression we would hear in opposition to any proposed code to protect the "religious" or the "patriotic" from "offense" and "incivility." Yet what deafening silence we have heard, in these times, in the campus acceptance of the speech provisions of so-called harassment codes.

"The purpose of speech codes . . . is to suppress speech, and to privilege one partisan, ideological view of the world."

The goal of a speech code, then, is to suppress speech one doesn't like, The goal of liberty and equal justice is to permit us to live in a complex but peaceful world of difference, disagreement, debate, moral witness, and efforts of persuasion without coercion and violence. Liberty and legal equality are hard-won, precious, and, indeed, because the social world is often discomforting, profoundly complex and troublesome ways of being human. They require, for their sustenance, men and women who would abhor their own power of censorship and their own special legal privileges as much as they abhor those of others. In enacting and enforcing speech codes, universities, for their own partisan reasons, have chosen to betray the human vision of freedom and legal equality. It was malignant to impose or permit such speech codes; to deny their oppressive effects while living in the midst of those effects is beyond the moral pale.

On virtually any college campus, for all of its rules of "civility" and all of its prohibitions of "hostile environment," assimilationist black men and women live daily with the terms "Uncle Tom" and "Oreo" said with impunity, while their tormenters live with special protections from offense. White students daily hear themselves, their friends, and their parents denounced as "racists" and "oppressors," while their tormenters live with special protections from offense. Believing Christians hear their beliefs ridiculed and see their sacred symbols traduced—virtually nothing, in the name of freedom, may not be said against them in the classroom, at rallies, and in personal encounters—while their tormenters live with special protection from offense. Men hear their sex abused, find themselves blamed for all the evils of the world, and enter classrooms whose very goal is to make them feel discomfort, while their tormenters live with special protections from "a hostile environment." The purpose of speech codes—patriotically orthodox or politically orthodox—is to suppress speech, and to privilege one partisan, ideological view of the world. Ideally, for the purposes of oppression, the very threat of the code suffices. When that does not suffice, those codes are, indeed, invoked.

Books Are Often Banned

by Persis M. Karim

About the author: *Persis M. Karim is an assistant professor of English at San Jose State University in California.*

How does a society that vigorously and sacredly regards its right to freedom of speech, so willingly and unquestioningly engage in censorship on a regular basis? The answer, of course, is that *book-banning*, the most widespread form of censorship in the U.S. today, is aimed specifically at children, and is successfully practiced using the rationale that we are protecting the youth of this country from the potentially dangerous effects of the ideas and representations contained within these so-called undesirable books. While the arguments supporting the banning of certain books in elementary and high school curricula and school libraries range from charges that a book is pornographic to "full of gross evils" to "undermining parental authority" and something as vague as "lacking literary merit," the reality is that the criteria for banning has more to do with parents, and political and religious organizations, than with the children themselves. Ironically, while hundreds of books are removed from course lists and libraries every year, children can watch television (unmediated by adults) that is chockful of sex and violence with only the condition that the network label the program at the top left corner of the screen with one of the several ratings that indicates the appropriateness of its contents for young viewers.

Why Books Are Considered Dangerous

How and why, you might be asking, is this all possible? What makes a book a potentially more dangerous medium than television? I want to begin by suggesting that speech acts—defined as speaking, writing, and public expression presumably protected under the First Amendment—are significantly different from the private world of thought which is encompassed by reading. This is only vaguely guarded by a notion of "intellectual freedom" which is not widely recognized and is certainly not extended to children. There really is no amendment that protects our right to have access to information and this may be one of the reasons why the practice of banning or challenging books so readily

Reprinted from Persis M. Karim, "The New Assault on Libraries," an online article from http://bookwire.bowker.com/bookinfo/article.aspx?2694, September 20, 1997. Reprinted with permission from the author.

takes place. Rather than being thought of as a violation of free speech, bans and challenges to books in schools and libraries are usually considered a protective measure for children who might otherwise be exposed willy-nilly to potentially "dangerous" and "offensive" materials.

Obviously, the danger is not in the actual act of reading itself, but rather, the possibility that the texts children read will incite questions, introduce novel ideas, and provoke critical inquiry. This wasn't always the case, however. Most challenges to and bans of books prior to the 1970s were primarily focused on a concern over obscenity and explicit sexuality. A smaller percentage of books like Harper Lee's *To Kill a Mockingbird* were challenged or banned because of how they might depict a particular group or community. The more concerted ideological attacks on materials in the schools began in the late 1970s with the founding and rise of a number of right-wing political action groups. Among them were Jerry Falwell's Moral Majority (later called the Liberty Foundation); Mel and Norma Gabler's Educational Research Analysts; the Eagle Forum led by Phyllis Schlafly; Concerned Women for America headed by Beverly La Haye; Citizens for Excellence in Education founded by Robert Simonds; and Pat Robertson's Christian Coalition. These groups and individuals began challenging books based not on dirty words and depictions of sex, but because of the representation of "a criticism, explicit or otherwise, of free-enterprise, patriotic, or fundamentalist Christian dogma."

Minority Authors Are Targeted

The attack on books because of their content and ideas, in fact, has everything to do with the way that changes in the public schools have reflected a greater emphasis on access to information. A greater emphasis on a twentieth-century American-focused curriculum in lieu of a nineteenth-century British one, has meant that literature and ideas that were previously considered too controversial or that simply reflected a range of U.S. cultures, interests, and historical movements (other than those of white and middle-class culture), have been introduced to students in school curricula and in libraries. Books written from the point of view of Blacks, Chicanos, Asians, and, of course, those books that reflect the perspective of women and homosexuals, have introduced new ideas and perspectives and have forced us to consider other truths. But these books have also generated

> "Book-banning, *the most widespread form of censorship in the U.S. today, is aimed specifically at children.*"

discomfort and anxiety because they are perceived by some as destabilizing what too often get labeled as "family values"; this is a euphemistic way of saying that these books and their authors threaten a particular view of this society that is and should be free of conflicts of race, gender, and class.

Banned and Challenged Books 1995–96 shows a disproportionate number of books written by black, Chicano, and homosexual authors represented on its pages; these books are frequently the target of campaigns by parents and right-wing groups which claim these books are unfit to be read and taught to children in schools. Challenges to and bans on books in the U.S. are motivated by the fear that these books will threaten someone's authority—that of a parent, a teacher, a state, an ideology, a lifestyle, or that these books and those who read and teach them won't be learning or teaching the "right" kind of values to maintain that authority. This is, of course, nothing new in human history—the lives of such thinkers as Socrates and Galileo adequately demonstrate this fact. But whereas in some other societies writers and thinkers are censored, arrested, jailed, or even put to death, in the U.S., we don't arrest the author, we merely make it difficult, and in some cases, impossible to read and/or teach his or her books. Our censorship begins with restricting access to ideas and books.

> *"Challenges to and bans on books in the U.S. are motivated by the fear that these books will threaten someone's authority."*

The New Attack on Libraries

The 1990s has seen the re-emergence and re-invigoration of Moral Majority-like organizations (the Christian Coalition is probably the most influential) whose largely right-wing agendas include a well-orchestrated campaign to challenge and remove books from the shelves of school and public libraries, ultimately making these books unpopular by making them less accessible and more difficult to introduce in classrooms. One such organization is the Family Friendly Libraries (FFL), founded by Karen Jo Gounaud, whose efforts are focused on trying to diminish the influence of the American Library Association (ALA) which Gounaud and her fellow members believe is pro-homosexuality, anti-family, and holds an all too radical position on most issues. Gounaud and the FLL see librarians' tolerance as masking a leftist political agenda and they believe the best way to target libraries is by utilizing a successful strategy of the right against liberal school boards: public campaigns to raise concern among parents, particularly suburban mothers, about the books their kids can read.

The struggle to determine the kinds of books that can be found in public libraries in some ways is a more aggressive campaign than the one waged in public schools over textbooks and novels used in the classroom. This may be because parents must place a measure of trust in the hands of teachers if they want their kids to succeed; sometimes parents and teachers see the work of organizations like the FLL as not only undercutting important civil liberties, but also as restricting debates over the quality and content of children's overall education. The library, however, is different than a classroom. It represents an unmediated, unsupervised space, where a child or adolescent is more or less free to wander among the shelves and check out those books that might not be available in school libraries or at home. The library in some ways is a more democratic and free space—those who use it do so voluntarily and can obtain books which represent a diverse spectrum of ideas and cultures.

Enter the FLL: In a September 1995 cover article of the Focus on the Family publication called *Citizen*, the FLL attacked the ALA for its policy of "unrestricted library access for youth" and its statement of "intellectual freedom" which declares that "a person's right to use a library should not be abridged because of origin, age, background or views." The FLL argues that this policy is the ALA's cover for "encouraging kids to read books that laud gay lifestyles, explore atheism or otherwise undermine families." Gounaud's organization has been receiving resources from a variety of like-minded "pro-family" organizations who see the battle against "free" access to libraries as the new frontier for their campaign to challenge, ban and restrict books which they see as undercutting the central "importance and superiority of the traditional family—mother and father married to each other . . ." (FLL charter). Rather than taking a neutral position toward the "traditional-family structure and family values," the FLL believes that libraries and librarians should promote them. Gounaud and the FLL intend to carry out this objective through a campaign whereby parents, rather than a direct act of political or governmental intervention (such as the banning of books in schools) restrict children's access to books in libraries.

"Restriction" (of access) rather than removal of books reflects the revised strategy of the FLL and other right-wing organizations who want to avoid charges of censorship. One way to do this, according to the FLL, is to have parents take books off the shelves which they consider offensive and adult in content, and to check them out indefinitely. Another proposal by the FLL is to restrict children's access to books by making the borrowing records of children accessible to parents. The rationale for this is, of course, that if the FLL can't change the culture of ideas and books in a library, they should "protect children" from what they consider to be the harmful effects of that culture. The ALA has naturally taken a strong position not only against this kind of intervention in children's rights to read free of parental or adult policing, but it has also tried to provide its librarians and library users with a campaign of education to support people's First Amendment rights and their intellectual freedom. When parents begin policing libraries and their children's reading and borrowing patterns, they have effectively made the banning and removal of books unnecessary. If you make children afraid of the consequences of reading and asking questions, you make them so leery of a place like a library, that they no longer want to go there. This, in my opinion, consti-

> *"If you make children afraid of the consequences of reading and asking questions, you make them . . . leery of a place like a library."*

tutes the more heinous aspect of censorship: making children and young people afraid to read, question, criticize—all necessary and fundamental aspects of maintaining anything that can be called a democracy.

So, when you commemorate Banned Books Week [an event sponsored by the ALA and other organizations], make a special effort to acknowledge your local public library, by paying it a visit. Bring your children and your neighbors' children with you and let them wander freely in the direction and toward the books that most attract them. Let them look at books that you never had the opportunity to read when you were a child or books that would never have even been published let alone written when you were their age. Let them come to understand that their right to free speech is nothing without the right to read, explore, and gaze into the vast universe of ideas and experiences contained within a library. It is, after all, one of the few places where the mind can run free.

The Teaching of Evolution Is Censored

by Leon Lynn

About the author: *Leon Lynn is an education journalist in Milwaukee.*

More than 70 years after the Scopes "Monkey Trial," the scientific theory of evolution is still too hot for some American schools to handle.

In that infamous 1925 case, worldwide attention focused on John T. Scopes, who was on trial for teaching evolution and breaking a Tennessee law which banned teaching "any theory that denies the story of the Divine Creation of man as taught in the Bible." Despite decades of scientific advances supporting evolution since the Scopes trial, despite numerous court rulings aimed at protecting science and educators from religious zealotry, and despite ever-increasing rhetoric about helping students compete in the modern world by giving them the best possible science education, schools all across the country are under pressure to downplay, ignore, or distort one of the fundamental theories of modern science. In at least some of those schools, the pressure is working.

Growing Attacks on Evolution

What's more, some observers say, the pressure is getting worse. Right-wingers and religious fundamentalists have been buoyed by newfound political strength in recent years. They are attacking evolution—as well as the whole concept of a secular, publicly funded school system—with ever-increasing vigor as they attempt to batter down the U.S. Constitution's separation of church and state and stamp their own brand of religion upon school curriculum.

Creationists don't often win outright victories; a court decision or legislative vote eventually stops many anti-evolution proposals. Nonetheless, the enemies of evolution often succeed in sending a message to teachers: If you value your careers, don't teach this. And many teachers, fearing they'll be fired or that their communities will shun them, comply.

Furthermore, in recent years creationists have adopted more sophisticated tactics. In particular, they have repackaged creationism to make such beliefs ap-

Reprinted from Leon Lynn, "The Evolution of Creationism," *Rethinking Schools*, Winter 1997–1998. Reprinted with permission from *Rethinking Schools*.

pear as legitimate scientific theory—which they then argue should be taught in conjunction with evolution.

Comparing Evolution and Creationism

Simply put, evolution is the scientific theory that all life forms on earth today are descended from a single cell, or at most a very few different cells. The diversity we see among species is the result of biological changes that have taken place over many hundreds of millions of years. During that time, new variations of plants and animals have appeared, through what the National Association of Biology Teachers terms "an unsupervised, impersonal, unpredictable, and natural process of temporal descent. . . ." Those new variations best able to adapt—to find food, escape predators, protect living space, or produce offspring—survived to pass along their traits to future generations. This is the process that Charles Darwin termed "natural selection" in his seminal 1859 work, "On the Origin of Species by Means of Natural Selection."

The scientific community attaches great importance to the theory of evolution. The National Association of Biology Teachers says it's impossible to provide "a rational, coherent and scientific account" of the history and diversity of organisms on earth, or to effectively teach cellular and molecular biology, without including the principles and mechanisms of evolution. Similarly, leading national voices for the reform of science education, including the National Science Teachers Association and the American Association for the Advancement of Science, emphasize the importance of teaching evolution as part of a well-rounded K-12 science curriculum. An NSTA position paper on evolution, for example, notes that there is "abundant and consistent evidence from astronomy, physics, biochemistry, geochronology, geology, biology, anthropology, and other sciences that evolution has taken place," making it an important "unifying concept for science." Scientific disciplines "with a historical component, such as astronomy, geology, biology, and anthropology, cannot be taught with integrity if evolution is not emphasized," NSTA concludes.

Generally, there's no conflict today between the theory of evolution and the religious beliefs of people who think that a supernatural entity guided the creation of the world. Many scientists and philosophers who accept the validity of evolution are nevertheless devoutly religious. Even Pope John Paul II, in a statement released in

> *"The enemies of evolution often succeed in sending a message to teachers: If you value your careers, don't teach this."*

1996, said that while the Catholic church holds that God created heaven and Earth, there is strong scientific evidence to support evolution.

In the realm of U.S. politics and education, however, the term "creationist" is generally used to refer to people actively pushing a particular, fundamentalist Christian religious perspective which rejects the theory of evolution as false.

While there are different factions—some creationists insist that Earth is only a few thousand years old, for example, while others remain open to the possibility that it's much older—people actively challenging evolution and seeking to promote creationism generally believe that:

• Life appeared on Earth suddenly, in forms similar or identical to those seen today. Humans, therefore, did not evolve from earlier species.

• All life was designed for certain functions and purposes.

• The Bible is an accurate historical record of creation and other events, such as the Great Flood. (Again, however, there are factional differences. Some creationists insist that the "creation week" was a literal seven-day week, while others believe the creation period could have lasted longer.)

Many creationists also believe that because evolution contradicts their interpretation of the Bible, it is therefore anti-God. For example Henry Morris, founder of a leading creationist think tank, the Institute for Creation Research, has written that evolution is dangerous because it leads "to the notion that each person owns himself, and is the master of his own destiny." This, he argues, is "contrary to the Bible teaching that man is in rebellion against God."

In the decades immediately following the publication of Darwin's landmark book in 1859, colleges began revising their curricula "to purge religious influences," says Gerald R. Skoog, a professor of education at Texas Tech University and a past president of the National Science Teachers Association. High schools

> *"In recent decades, numerous state and federal court decisions have sought to protect scientists and educators who advocate the teaching of evolution."*

began following suit around 1900, but the process was by no means swift or comprehensive. In 1925 in Dayton, Tennessee, science teacher John T. Scopes was put on trial for breaking Tennessee's law banning the teaching of evolution. The case became an international spectacle because of the appearances, and impassioned arguments, of lawyer Clarence Darrow on Scopes' behalf and political giant William Jennings Bryan in opposition to evolution. Scopes was convicted, although his conviction was later dismissed on appeal by the state Supreme Court. The anti-evolution law remained on the books in Tennessee until 1967, when it was finally repealed.

Protection by the Courts

In recent decades, numerous state and federal court decisions have sought to protect scientists and educators who advocate the teaching of evolution. At the heart of the decisions is the courts' view that banning the teaching of evolution is a violation of the U.S. Constitution's separation of church and state. Among the more significant decisions:

• The U.S. Supreme Court ruled in 1968 that an Arkansas law banning the teaching of evolution was unconstitutional. In essence, the court held that creationists were attempting to foist a particular religious philosophy in the schools.

• In 1981 the Supreme Court rejected a California creationist's claim that classroom discussions of evolution infringed on his right, and the rights of his children, to free exercise of religion.

• In 1987, the Supreme Court tossed out a Louisiana law that required the teaching of creationism whenever evolution was taught in schools, saying the law was an endorsement of religion.

• In 1990, the Seventh Circuit Court of Appeals ruled that a school district could prohibit a teacher from teaching creationism and that such a prohibition wouldn't violate the teacher's free-speech rights.

• Similarly, in 1994 the Ninth Circuit Court of Appeals ruled that a teacher's First Amendment right to free exercise of religion is not violated by a school-district requirement that teachers include evolution in biology curricula.

> *"Right-wing lawmakers are carrying out attacks on public education on numerous fronts, with an eye toward pushing a fundamentalist political agenda."*

• In September 1997, a U.S. district court in Louisiana struck down as unconstitutional a three-year-old policy in Tangipahoa Parish that required teachers to read a disclaimer before teaching the theory of evolution.

Evolution also received a major boost, oddly enough, from the Soviet Union's launch of Sputnik in 1957. Critics of the U.S. education system seized on the launch, saying America's "defeat" in the space race was due to poor schooling. This issue quickly became part of the national political agenda, and schools began putting new emphasis on math and science education.

Despite these court decisions, however, and the resurgence of interest in science education that flowed from the space race, evolution remains a popular target in school board meeting rooms, legislative halls, and courthouses from Virginia to California. The last decade in particular has seen a surge in creationist political activity.

Right-Wing Activism

"It certainly looks as though it's on the rise," says Eugenie Scott, executive director of the National Center for Science Education, which advocates the teaching of evolution and opposes allowing creationism in schools. "I think the increase can be largely attributed to religious conservatives getting elected to school boards," she says. "It only takes one or two creationists on a school board to generate significant controversy, especially if the science curriculum undergoes periodic review."

Religious right groups like the Christian Coalition and Citizens for Excellence in Education have pushed hard to get right-wing Christians elected to local school boards in recent years. That's because school-board elections often elicit jaw-droppingly low voter turnout, making it easier for a small but motivated faction to elect its hand-picked candidate. School boards are also attractive to right-wingers because board members have—or at least appear to have—tremendous influence over what can and can't be taught in a community's schools.

Right-wing political activists also got a tremendous boost in 1994, when an electorate disenchanted with Bill Clinton voted an unprecedented number of Republicans into state-level and local offices. The legislatures in many states slid rightward literally overnight. Today, right-wing lawmakers are carrying out attacks on public education on numerous fronts, with an eye toward pushing a fundamentalist political agenda—regardless of the wishes of most parents, teachers, and educators—and eroding the separation of church and state that has long been the hallmark of public schools. In addition to creationism, major battles are being waged around the country on such issues as school prayer, school-sponsored religious activity, so-called "parental-rights initiatives," sex education, and vouchers. Carole Shields, president of People for the American Way, has called these attacks on public education "one element of the Right's attack on the fundamental institutions and values of American society. In attacking the schools, the Right is taking aim at the fundamental notion of opportunity for all. . . . What better way to deny real opportunity could be devised than to hamper the institutions that furnish children with an education?"

Examples of creationists trying to use their political might to foist their religious beliefs on public schools include:

• In Vista, California, in 1992, voters elected a school board member who was also an accountant for the Institute for Creation Research. After the district's teachers rejected his suggestion to use the creationist book *Of Pandas and People* as a science textbook, he began advocating that teachers teach "weaknesses in evolution" whenever evolution was taught. Eventually, the board member and two others who had consistently voted with him on such issues were recalled.

> *"Even when creationists seem to lose a struggle, . . . the controversy they generate can leave teachers wary to so much as mention evolution to their students."*

• In Alabama in 1995, the state school board voted 6–1 in favor of inserting a disclaimer into biology textbooks. Written by the right-wing Eagle Forum, it reads in part: "This textbook discusses evolution, a controversial theory some scientists present as a scientific explanation for the origin of living things. . . . No one was present when life first appeared on earth. Therefore, any statement about life's origins should be considered as theory, not fact." According to People for the American Way, Alabama Governor Fob James, who is president of the state school board, urged the board to accept the motion, saying: "If one wanted to know something about the origin of life you might want to look at Genesis and you can get the whole story, period." James also used his discretionary funds to purchase and send more than 900 copies of "Darwin on Trial," a creationist book, to all biology teachers in the state.

• In Hall County, Georgia, in 1996, the school board adopted a resolution directing the textbook and curriculum committee to include materials in the science curriculum that explain and discuss creationism. The board rescinded this resolution after the state attorney general warned that this would be unconstitutional.

• In Tennessee in 1996, the Senate and House education committees both approved a bill that would have allowed schools to fire any teacher who presented evolution as a fact. A Senate amendment "defined" evolution as an "unproven belief that random, undirected forces produced a world of living things." Debate over the bill continued for months, despite an opinion issued by the state attorney general saying that the bill was unconstitutional. It was finally voted down by the Legislature.

A Struggle in Tennessee

Wesley Roberts, an ecology and environmental sciences teacher in Nashville, got himself—and his students—involved in the struggle to kill the Tennessee bill. He attended several sessions of the Legislature during the debates, sometimes bringing students from his school with him. "I think they (the students) were smart enough to realize that their teachers were about to be censored," he says, "and regardless of their position on creation and evolution, they did not like that at all." The students "definitely had an impact on the debate," he says. "The media were all over them, interviewing them. They loved getting sound bites from angry kids and plastering them all over TV and the newspaper."

While the rejection of the bill was "a real victory," Roberts says, it will take much more to really pave the way for evolution to be taught in Tennessee. Many teachers, mindful of all the ill will focused on evolution for so long, "won't even mention it in class," he says. Even students in his advanced-placement environmental science class "have very rarely had any instruction in evolution." In fact, in a class Roberts teaches at a nearby college, "I always ask my students how much instruction they've had in evolution, and it's always the case that if they've had it, they went to a private school or they're from the North," he says.

This "chilling effect" stifles teachers all across the country, North as well as South. Even when creationists seem to lose a struggle, as in Tennessee, the controversy they generate can leave teachers wary to so much as mention evolution to their students. "There's a tendency for teachers to be noncombative," says Scott of the National Center for Science Education. "Generally teachers are not looking for a fight. . . . If they perceive that a subject is going to get them in trouble, they may very well decide to just steer clear."

New Creationist Strategies

Despite suffering some political and judicial setbacks, anti-evolutionists are not about to give up applying that pressure. Leaders of the creationist movement have been industrious and relatively skillful about repackaging and reintroducing their beliefs.

Take, for example, the creationists' response to the 1987 U.S. Supreme Court decision, known as *Edwards v. Aguillar,* which struck down the Louisiana law requiring teachers to give equal time to "creation science" whenever they taught evolution. The late Justice William Brennan, writing the majority opinion, made it clear that "creation science" wasn't science at all, but an endorsement of faith-based religious belief. He also rejected the idea that the Louisiana law was promoting "a basic concept of fairness" by requiring that both evolution and creation science be taught. "Instead," he wrote, "this Act has the distinctly different purpose of discrediting evolution by counter-balancing its teaching at every turn with the teaching of creationism."

Brennan delivered a powerful rhetorical blow against anti-evolutionists. But deep in his 3,800-word opinion, creationists found a single sentence that gave them something they could build on. Brennan had written: "Teaching a variety of scientific theories about the origins of humankind to schoolchildren might be validly done with the clear secular intent of enhancing the effectiveness of science instruction." And in the dissenting opinion by Justice Antonin Scalia, they found another useful phrase: "The people of Louisiana, including those who are Christian fundamentalists, are quite entitled, as a secular matter, to have whatever scientific evidence there may be against evolution presented in their schools. . . ."

> *"Just because the theory of evolution is subject to continued testing and examination in light of new evidence doesn't make it untrue."*

These two statements set the stage for the two most current versions of creationism: the so-called "theory of intelligent design" and the efforts to inject "scientific evidence against evolution" into school curricula. Both are perhaps best exemplified by the creationist pseudo-textbook *Of Pandas and People.* Similar reasoning lurks behind the many efforts to slap disclaimers on science textbooks, reminding students that evolution is "only a theory" and not fact. This is a serious misuse of the scientific meaning of "theory," making it sound like a synonym for "guess" or "hunch." In fact, according to the National Association of Biology Teachers, "a (scientific) theory is not a guess or an approximation, but an extensive explanation developed from well-documented, reproducible sets of experimentally derived data from repeated observations of natural processes." In other words, just because the theory of evolution is subject to continued testing and examination in light of new evidence doesn't make it untrue.

Chapter 2

The reasons behind such attacks on evolution are obvious, according to a statement written by Rob Boston, a spokesman for the group Americans United for the Separation of Church and State. "They're shifting their attacks by trying to water down the teaching of evolution—put doubts in children's minds. They figure that if they can't get creationism taught in public schools, then the next best thing is to take the instruction about evolution and undercut it."

The Study of Creationism Is Censored

by Jerry Bergman

About the author: *Jerry Bergman is a professor of science at Northwest State College in Archbold, Ohio.*

The mass media commonly reports attempts to censor pornographic literature from libraries, yet rarely discusses a far more harmful form of library censorship, that of Christian or pro-moral works. Surveys consistently find that quality materials of recent copyright date favorable to the intelligent design world view are rarely found in American university, college, high school or public libraries.

Why Creationism Is Censored

Increased exposure to an idea improves the likelihood of its acceptance. A primary reason why some form of evolution is accepted by about half of the American population is because of the high level of public exposure that this belief receives in public schools and also on television, in magazines and elsewhere. Of 38 individuals interviewed as to why they accepted evolution, Jerry Bergman found that all but three had very limited knowledge about the theory. Most had simply assumed from their cultural exposure that the theory has been empirically demonstrated to be true. The theory of naturalistic evolution is most often not directly, but more often subtly, taught and assumed in textbooks to be an accurate view of reality. It is in this way that students learn about the theory, not by careful evaluation of the empirical evidence and logic for and against it. As [John] Eidsmoe notes:

> In public schools, evolutionary naturalism is commonly taught as fact. Zoos, museums, cultural exhibits and national parks proclaim the evolution of life and rigid uniformitarian geology. Despite pious claims of neutrality and equal access, public television presents Carl Sagan's "Cosmos" along with other evolutionary programs, while ignoring the other side. The public is bombarded with evolutionary thought wherever they turn—much of it at the taxpayers' expense.

Excerpted from Jerry Bergman, "Censorship of Information on Origins," *Creation Ex Nihilo Technical Journal*, November 3, 1996. Reprinted with permission from *Creation Ex Nihilo Technical Journal*, a ministry of Answers in Genesis. For more information, visit www.answersingenesis.com.

A major reason for this one-sided differential exposure that exists in the secular world is that pro-creationist materials and information are heavily censored from the public domain. If it is discussed, the discussion is not uncommonly limited to a polemical diatribe littered with ad hominem arguments. Anti-creationists rarely define the term creation, thus it is not easy to know who they dislike. They use much name-calling and value laden words such as pseudo-science, religious, or Bible-thumpers. The problem of blatant censorship of pro-creationist material is worldwide in its extent and effect. [Ken] Ham stated that in Australia a librarian . . . wrote to us concerning the magazine *Ex Nihilo,* which was sent to the school as a gift subscription, from a concerned parent. . . . Part of her letter reads as follows, "As the person responsible for selection of resources available from the school library, I . . . [request] your subscription officer remove the school's address from your current mailing list. Further, if other gift subscriptions arrive, please ignore them."

Ham's comments on this situation are as follows:

"Surely, the materials in a public school library should make available all possible . . . resources to the students and teachers. To allow one person's beliefs to ban this publication from the school library, and not even allow others to have it for consideration in their research, is a dangerous precedent."

Examples of Censorship

Individual examples such as these illustrate a problem which all surveys demonstrate is widespread and pervasive. [Jim] Melnick concluded that:

> Creationist literature has been self-censored from nearly every major secular university library in America. An OCLC computer search . . . indicated that of the over 3,000 institutions on the OCLC list, only 33 subscribed to the *Creation Research Society Quarterly,* [which is] without question the preeminent journal in the field of scientific creationism and read throughout the world. When one subtracts all the Bible colleges and seminaries . . . barely enough other schools [are] left to count . . . [Creationist A.E.] Wilder-Smith, who studied natural sciences at Oxford and holds three doctorates, recently published . . . a strictly scientific text which can stand up to any university work on evolution. It is currently available at only eighteen institutions on the OCLC's list. By contrast, Dorothy Nelkin's book, *Science Textbook Controversies and the Politics of Equal Time* . . . is already available at over four hundred institutions. Better examples could be cited.

> *"Pro-creationist materials and information are heavily censored from the public domain."*

The writer replicated Melnick's study and, although not as extensive, his basic conclusions were fully supported. I found, for example, that the only book in print on discrimination against creationists, *The Criterion,* as of November

1994, was in a grand total of five libraries of the 5,000 in the system—yet the few anti-creationist titles checked were in hundreds of libraries. In another study of censorship, Professor [Rick] Balogh concluded that:

"Creationist theories are censored in the schools, in the media, and in textbooks published by major publishers. Libraries, even if they want to, find it difficult to stock creationist books.". . .

Creationist Views Are Not Published

The censorship problem is well illustrated in the history of the publication of the high school textbook, *Biology: A Search for Order in Complexity,* which had the input of a dozen or so Ph.D.-level creationists. After approaching 15 textbook publishers, not one of them would even look at the manuscript! The textbook was finally published by Zondervan, an evangelical publisher. It sold well in Christian schools but made little headway in the public schools, although several states placed it on their "Approved" list.

Then various court decisions actually "banned" the book, and as a result, most school districts refused to even consider it. The book is void of open proselytizing and direct creationist content, and is very close in content to a standard biology textbook. A few statements infer that God's design can be seen in the structures the text discusses, but the text as a whole is well balanced, even briefly explaining evolution theory fairly well. Yet, because it was written by creationists and tried to look at both sides, it was banned in many states.

> *"It is almost unknown for an outspoken creationist to publish in leading journals."*

To be fair, although problems are common, there have always been some publishers that accept creationist material. One is a Phi Delta Kappa monograph in the prestigious fastback series on creation/evolution (Phi Delta Kappa is the honor society in education) which the writer published. Dorothy Allford, a medical doctor, published *Instant Creation—Not Evolution* with Stein and Day, and Putnam published a work edited by [John] Monsma, *Behind the Dim Unknown.* The chapter authors include Duane Gish, Russell Artist and George Howe, although several progressive creationists are included. Philosophical Library has also published several creationist books—not surprising in that they publish a wide variety of literature, from good science to far-out pseudo-science.

Nonetheless, this does not negate the fact that, in general, extreme censorship exists. In spite of it, or because of this problem, [Henry] Morris claims that the average publication record of creationists is the same as non-creationists in areas not relating to creationism, or their creationist conclusions must be heavily disguised. Morris also claims that the Institute for Creation Research (ICR) staff publication record is typical of creationists worldwide, and that their ten scientists ". . . have published at least 150 research papers and ten books in their own scientific fields—all in standard, scientific, refereed journals or through secular book publishers—in addition to hundreds of creationist articles and perhaps 50 books in creationism and related fields."

A Survey of Creationist Articles

The extensive literature review by [Henry] Cole and [Eugenie] Scott also found that creationists publish science research in their field, but only non-creationist articles. Because these researchers publish in non-creation areas, often prolifically, demonstrates that they are competent and that articles espousing creationism clearly are censored. A few creationists, though, have actually been able to have openly creationist works published in secular journals. Dudley Whitney, an editor of various agricultural journals who later became a creationist, ". . . was also one of the few creationists in modern time who was able to get solidly scientific, frankly creationist, articles in established journals. In 1935, he published an article defending a young earth in the prestigious *Annual Report of the Committee on Geologic Time,* the paper having been invited by Dr. Alfred C. Lane, the eminent geologist."

"Interestingly though, the publication of these frankly creationist articles," according to Morris, resulted in "such a prejudicial reaction that the journal finally had to close down." Unfortunately, Cole and Scott's statement is all too true: "Creationists frequently claim that they do conduct research that supports . . . creationism. They argue that the scientific establishment that controls the selection of articles for the major journals is biased against their views. Thus . . . evidence for the unpopular view is suppressed."

In an examination of all literature printed in secular magazines about creationism from 1971 to 1994, a grand total of four articles out of over 4,000 were located which defended creationism, all of which were followed by one or more articles which tried to "refute" the article supporting creationism. One appeared in *Phi Delta Kappa,* others in *Academia, Creation/Evolution* and *Science Digest.* The above literature search was not able to locate a single article in any secular magazine which defended the civil rights of creationists.

Some creationists even have articles accepted which are never published after the publisher found out who they were. A reviewer of one article said "Best article on topic I've ever seen!" yet it was rescinded. One journal even compiles a list of creationists from letters to the editor and other sources such as *Creation Research*

"Probably one of the most serious and common areas of censorship . . . is from textbooks."

Society Quarterly articles. Many creationists publish extensively but most all are closet creationists, and it is almost unknown for an outspoken creationist to publish in leading journals. Their papers are rejected by a "referee process" which is often actually a board of censors. Many editors openly admit that they will not publish a paper that does not conform to their world view. . . .

Probably one of the most serious and common areas of censorship of support for the intelligent design world view and theism in general is from textbooks. The writer's review of over 200 textbooks found virtually all of them assume *a priori* that God does not exist, rarely adopting even the agnostic position. A textbook he used for several terms, *Anthropology,* by [Carol] Ember and [Melvin] Ember assumed both atheism and "reverse creationism," that is, humans created God, not the other way around. Not giving credence to even the agnostic view, the textbook teaches that God is a human creation thought up to explain that which cannot yet be explained by science (and when science fills the gap, the need for God will evaporate completely, the authors argue). The only valid question is how and why we created Him.

Several theories have been developed to answer these two questions. One says that we created God out of a "psychological need" for a mental crutch to help us deal with the insecurities of life and explain certain events, such as the universe's existence. Another view is that "the God belief" is functional because it unifies society, facilitating social harmony and societal bonds which reduce the likelihood of suicide and other problems that stem from [sociologist Emile] Durkheim's concept of anomie. Another theory of why humans created God was developed by Karl Marx and teaches that the idea of God is used by the powerful to control the powerless.

> *"Theism is commonly ridiculed and criticized, or at least is given little credence."*

The only legally acceptable position for American public schools would be to take the agnostic view. This view would note that some people believe that God exists, others deny this belief. In this view, religion is seen as a cultural universal. Hypotheses about why religion exists could include the interaction of humans and God allowed humans to have learned about Him.

An example would be that which is learned through revelation as recorded in the Scriptures. Since all persons came from Adam (who clearly knew that God created him) this belief would be a universal heritage, modified only by time and local conditions. Thus, religion would be a cultural universal for this reason. This option could be presented in addition to the reverse creationism position, helping the text be fair and balanced by presenting both sides.

The Prevalence of Atheism

In endeavoring to find a philosophy book suitable for a Christian college, I was unable to locate a single one which presented even an agnostic position! All argued either vigorously or subtly (which is more pernicious because the indoctrination is less blatant, thus more palatable) for atheism. I have also never been able to find a suitable biology text for my college class in this area—all of them I have examined directly or indirectly teach atheism. This is clearly unconstitutional, yet is the norm in higher education. Not only do the textbooks argue for atheism, but in the writer's college classes, his science, and even philosophy professors almost without exception argued, at times vigorously, for atheism. Theism is commonly ridiculed and criticized, or at least is given little credence.

A text I finally selected, *Philosophy and Introduction of the Art of Wondering* by Dr. Christian concludes that four "wild dragons" exist which man could not explain for eons, and thus resorted to the concept of God. These wild dragons—the origin of life, man, matter, and the universe—have now been "tamed" by science. We now understand, he concludes, where life and humans came from, and no longer need to resort to a God hypothesis. And these explanations are, the book argues, more than a hypothesis. Quoting Cyril Ponnamperuma (who won a Nobel prize for his work) he concludes,

> "We now know that once the right molecules accumulated at the right time and the right arrangement, life could begin almost instantaneously."

Is this not openly atheistic apologetics?—not to mention openly false. Nothing close to life has ever been created in the lab by the world's most talented scientists working with billions of dollars of equipment. Evolution is assumed throughout the text to be factual (and this is not even a biology text), and is constantly referred to as the explanation for not only life, but for the existence of the universe itself. As "we have demonstrated that life evolves, both the early stages and to man, belief in the Creator is," the text concludes, "unnecessary." It blatantly concludes that evolution is mankind's creator, not God. "It produced him according to its criteria . . . [our] environment is the creator; man is the creature." In the words of [M. Stanton] Evans:

> Sources of hostility to religious belief in modern thought and politics are not far to seek; familiar enough, we may assume, not to require a long discussion. . . . The . . . notion that religious faith is merely superstition and thus irrelevant to the world we live in, since its precepts have been supplanted or discredited by "science." All religions, in this view, are mystical efforts to explain things that have natural causes not yet deduced by reason. This too has been a leading feature of modern thought in virtually all its aspects. Such thinking is powerfully aided by the belief that Darwinian evolution offers scientific answers to questions about human life that were previously sought for in the counsels of religion. . . .

Responding to Censorship

It has been documented that both discrimination and censorship against creationists are extremely common, especially in academia. A major response to deal with this problem is first awareness, and then to endeavor to be vigilant in dealing with individual issues as they arise at the local level. Secular humanists have responded in this way with a high level of success. Many libraries now contain pornographic literature, openly accessible to all patrons, that was illegal to distribute only a few years ago. Their activity and vigilance in this area has produced this state of affairs. Likewise, the censorship against creationists must be dealt with in similar ways. This situation must be understood for what it is—religious bigotry and intolerance.

Campuses Should Restrict Racist Speech

by Richard Delgado and Jean Stefancic

About the authors: *Richard Delgado is the Jean Lindsley Professor of Law at the University of Colorado. Jean Stefancic is a research associate at the University of Colorado School of Law.*

The First Amendment appears to stand as a formidable barrier to campus rules prohibiting group-disparaging speech. Designed to assure that debate on public issues is "uninhibited, robust, and wide open," the First Amendment protects speech that we hate as much as that which we hold dear. Yet racial insults implicate powerful social interests in equality and equal personhood. When uttered on university campuses, racial insults bring into play additional concerns. Few would question that the university has strong, legitimate interests in teaching students and teachers to treat each other respectfully; protecting minority-group students from harassment; and protecting diversity, which could be impaired if students of color become demoralized and leave the university, or if parents of minority race decide to send their children elsewhere.

Exceptions to Free Speech

Only on one occasion has the United States Supreme Court weighed free speech against the equal-protection values endangered by race-hate speech. In *Beauharnais v. Illinois*, the defendant was convicted under a statute prohibiting dissemination of materials promoting racial or religious hatred. Citing the "fighting words" doctrine of *Chaplinsky v. New Hampshire,* Justice [Felix] Frankfurter ruled that libelous statements aimed at groups, like those aimed at individuals, fall outside First Amendment protection. Later decisions, notably *New York Times v. Sullivan* and *R.A.V. v. St. Paul*, have increased protection for libelous speech, with the result that some commentators and courts question whether *Beauharnais* today would be decided differently. Yet, *Beauharnais* has never been overruled, and in the meantime many courts have afforded redress in tort for racially or sexually insulting language, with few finding any constitu-

Excerpted from Richard Delgado and Jean Stefancic, *Must We Defend Nazis?: Hate Speech, Pornography, and the New First Amendment*. Reprinted with permission from New York University Press.

tional problem with doing so.

Moreover, over the past century the courts have carved out or tolerated dozens of "exceptions" to free speech. These exceptions include speech used to form a criminal conspiracy or an ordinary contract; speech that disseminates an official secret; speech that defames or libels someone; speech that is obscene; speech that creates a hostile workplace; speech that violates a trademark or plagiarizes another's words; speech that creates an immediately harmful impact or is tantamount to shouting "fire" in a crowded theater; "patently offensive" speech directed at captive audiences or broadcast on the airwaves; speech that constitutes "fighting words"; speech that disrespects a judge, teacher, military officer, or other authority figure; speech used to defraud a consumer; words used to fix prices; words ("stick 'em up—hand over the money") used to communicate a criminal threat; and untruthful or irrelevant speech given under oath or during a trial.

Much speech, then, is unprotected. The issues are whether the social interest in reining in racially offensive speech is as great as that which gives rise to these "exceptional" categories, and whether the use of racially offensive language has speech value. Because little recent Supreme Court law directly addresses these issues, one might look to the underlying policies of our system of free expression to understand how the Court may rule if an appropriate case comes before it. . . .

Racist Speech Is Divisive

Our system of free expression serves a number of societal and individual goals. Included are the personal fulfillment of the speaker; ascertainment of the truth; participation in democratic decision-making; and achieving a balance between social stability and change. Applying these policies to the controversy surrounding campus anti-racism rules yields little support for their detractors. Uttering racial slurs may afford the racially troubled speaker some immediate relief, but hardly seems essential to self-fulfillment in any ideal sense. Indeed, social science writers hold that making racist remarks impairs, rather than promotes, the growth of the person who makes them, by encouraging rigid, dichotomous thinking and impeding moral development. Moreover, such remarks serve little dialogic purpose; they do not seek to connect the speaker and addressee in a community of shared ideals. They divide, rather than unite.

Additionally, slurs contribute little to the discovery of truth. Classroom discussion of racial matters and even the speech of a bigot aimed at prov-

"Few would question that the university has strong, legitimate interests in teaching students and teachers to treat each other respectfully."

ing the superiority of the white race might move us closer to the truth. But one-on-one insults do not. They neither state nor attack a proposition; they are like a slap in the face. By the same token, racial insults do little to help reach broad social consensuses. Indeed, by demoralizing their victim they may actually reduce speech, dialogue, and participation in political life. "More speech" is rarely a solution. Epithets often strike suddenly, immobilizing their victim and rendering her speechless. Often they are delivered in cowardly, anonymous fashion—in the form of a defaced poster or leaflet slipped under a student's door, or hurled by a group against a single victim, rendering response foolhardy. Nor do they help strike a healthy balance between stability and social change. Racial epithets could be argued to relieve racial tension harmlessly and thus contribute to racial stability, but this strained argument has been called into question by social science.

Yet racial epithets are speech, and as such we ought to protect them unless there is a very good reason for not doing so. A recent book by Kent Greenawalt [*Speech, Crime and the Uses of Language*] suggests a framework for assessing laws against insults. Drawing on First Amendment principles and case law, Greenawalt writes that the setting, the speaker's intention, the forum's interest, and the relationship between the speaker and the victim must be considered. Moreover, abusive words (like kike, nigger, wop, and faggot) are punishable if spoken with intent, cause a harm capable of formulation in clear legal language, and form a message essentially devoid of ideas. Greenawalt offers as an example of words that could be criminally punishable, "You Spic whore," uttered by four men to a woman of color at a bus stop, intended to humiliate her. He notes that such words can have long-term damaging effects

> *"Racial insults do little to help reach broad social consensuses. Indeed, by demoralizing their victim they may actually reduce speech."*

on the victim and have little if any cognitive content; that meaning which the words convey may be expressed in other ways.

Under Greenawalt's test, narrowly drawn university guidelines penalizing racial slurs might well withstand scrutiny. The university forum has a strong interest in establishing a nonracist atmosphere. Moreover, most university rules are aimed at face-to-face remarks that are intentionally abusive. Most exclude classroom speech, speeches to a crowd, and satire published in a campus newspaper. Under Greenawalt's nonabsolutist approach, such rules might well be held constitutional.

An Equal Protection View

The First Amendment perspective thus yields no clear-cut result. Society has a strong interest in seeing that expression is as unfettered as possible, yet racial slurs have no great social worth and can cause serious harm. Unfortunately, looking at the problem of racist speech from the perspective of the equality-protecting amendments yields no clearer result.

Equality and equal respect are highly valued principles in our system of jurisprudence. Three constitutional provisions and a myriad of federal and state statutes are aimed at protecting the rights of racial, religious, and sexual minorities to be free from discrimination in housing, education, jobs, and many other areas of life. Moreover, universities have considerable power to enact regulations protecting minority interests. Yet the equality principle is not without limits. State agencies may not redress breaches by means that too broadly encroach on the rights of

> *"Rules bridling racist speech will be found constitutional if there is a local history of racial disruption."*

whites, or on other constitutional principles. Rigorous rules of intent, causation, standing, and limiting relief circumscribe what may be done. New causes of action are not lightly recognized; for example, the legal system has resisted efforts by feminists to have pornography deemed a civil rights offense against women. . . . Even tort law has been slow to recognize a civil cause of action for racist speech.

Moreover, courts have held or implied that a university's power to effectuate campus policies, presumably including equality, is also limited. Cases stemming from efforts to regulate the wearing of armbands, what students may publish in the school newspaper, or their freedom to gather in open areas for worship or speech have shown that individual liberty will sometimes limit an institution's interest in achieving its educational objectives—students do not abandon all their constitutional rights at the schoolhouse door. According to the author of a leading treatise on higher-education law, rules bridling racist speech will be found constitutional if there is a local history of racial disruption; if the rules are narrowly tailored to punish only face-to-face insults and avoid encroaching on classroom and other protected speech; if they are consistently and evenhandedly applied; and if due process protections such as the right to representation and a fair hearing are present. The author's guidelines seem plausible, but have yet to be tested. One set of rules was promulgated, then withdrawn; others were declared overly broad and subsequently redrafted. In several jurisdictions, the American Civil Liberties Union [ACLU] has announced that it is monitoring developments and may file suit.

In the meantime, analogous authority continues to develop. In *Bob Jones University v. United States,* the Supreme Court held that universities may not discriminate in the name of religion. In *University of Pennsylvania v. EEOC,* the Supreme Court held that a university's desire to protect confidential tenure files did not insulate the university from review in connection with discrimination investigations. Both cases imply that the anti-discrimination imperative will at times prevail over other strong interests, such as freedom of religion or academic freedom—and possibly speech. In the recent Minnesota "cross-burning" case, however, the Court held that criminal laws regulating hate messages must be broadly and neutrally drawn.

The Social Construction of Reality

As we have seen, neither the constitutional narrative of the First, nor of the Thirteenth and Fourteenth, Amendments clearly prevails in connection with campus anti-racism rules. Judges must choose. The dilemma is embedded in the nature of our system of law and politics: we want and fear both equality and liberty. We think the problem of campus anti-racism rules can yield to a postmodern insight: that speech by which society constructs a stigma picture of minorities may be regulated consistently with the First Amendment. Indeed, regulation may be necessary for full effectuation of the values of equal personhood we hold equally dear.

The first step is recognizing that racism is, in almost all its aspects, a class harm—the essence of which is subordination of one people by another. The mechanism of this subordination is a complex, interlocking series of acts, some physical, some symbolic. Although the physical acts (like lynchings and cross burnings) are often the most striking, the symbolic acts are the most insidious. By communicating and constructing a shared cultural image of the victim group as inferior, we enable ourselves to feel comfortable about the disparity in power and resources between ourselves and the stigmatized group. Even civil rights law may contribute to this stigmatization: the group is so vulnerable that it requires help. The shared picture also demobilizes the victims of discrimination, particularly the young. Indeed, social scientists have seen evidence of self-hatred and rejection of their own identity in children of color as early as age three.

The ubiquity and incessancy of harmful racial depiction are thus the source of its virulence. Like water dripping on sandstone, it is a pervasive harm which only the most hardy can resist. Yet the prevailing First Amendment paradigm predisposes us to treat racist speech as an individual harm, as though we had only to evaluate the effect of a single drop of water. This approach—corresponding to liberal, individualistic theories of self and society—systematically misperceives the experience of racism for both victim and perpetrator. This mistake is natural, and corresponds to one aspect of our natures—our individualistic selves. In this capacity, we want and need liberty. But we also exist in a social capacity; we need others to fulfill ourselves as beings. In this group aspect, we require inclusion, equality, and equal respect.

> *"Racist speech . . . works to disempower minority groups by crippling the effectiveness of their speech in rebuttal."*

Constitutional narratives of equal protection and prohibition of slavery—narratives that encourage us to form and embrace collectivity and equal citizenship for all—reflect this second aspect of our existence.

When the tacit consent of a group begins to coordinate the exercise of individual rights so as seriously to jeopardize participation by a smaller group, the "rights" nature of the first group's actions acquires a different character and dimension. The exercise of an individual right now poses a group harm and must be weighed against this qualitatively different type of threat.

Greenawalt's book has made a cautious move in this direction. Although generally a defense of free speech in its individual aspect, his book also notes that speech is a primary means by which we construct reality. Thus, a wealthy and well-regarded citizen who is victimized by a vicious defamation is able to recover in tort. His social "picture," in which he has a property interest, has been damaged, and will require laborious reconstruction. It would require only a slight extension of Greenawalt's observation to provide protection from racial slurs and hate speech. Indeed, the rich man has the dominant "story" on his side; repairing the defamation's damage will be relatively easy.

> *"Resurgent racism on our nation's campuses is rapidly becoming a national embarrassment."*

Racist speech, by contrast, is not so readily repaired—it separates the victim from the storytellers who alone have credibility. Not only does racist speech, by placing all the credibility with the dominant group, strengthen the dominant story, it also works to disempower minority groups by crippling the effectiveness of their speech in rebuttal. This situation makes free speech a powerful asset to the dominant group, but a much less helpful one to subordinate groups—a result at odds, certainly, with marketplace theories of the First Amendment. Unless society is able to deal with this incongruity, the Thirteenth and Fourteenth Amendments and our complex system of civil rights statutes will be of little avail. At best, they will be able to obtain redress for episodic, blatant acts of individual prejudice and bigotry. This redress will do little to alleviate the source of the problem: the speech that creates the stigma-picture that makes the acts hurtful in the first place, and that renders almost any other form of aid—social or legal—useless.

Racist Speech Is Different

Could judges and legislators effectuate our suggestion that speech which constructs a stigma-picture of a subordinate group stands on a different footing from sporadic speech aimed at persons who are not disempowered? It might be argued that all speech constructs the world to some extent, and that every speech act could prove offensive to someone. Traditionalists find modern art troublesome, Republicans detest left-wing speech, and some men hate speech that constructs a sex-neutral world. Yet race—like gender and a few other characteristics—is different; our entire history and culture bespeak this difference. Thus, judges easily could differentiate speech which subordinates blacks, for example, from that which disparages factory owners. Will they choose to do so? There is cause for doubt: low-grade racism benefits the status quo. Moreover, our system's winners have a stake in liberal, marketplace interpretations of law and politics—their seeming neutrality and meritocratic nature reassure the decision-makers that their social position is deserved.

Still, resurgent racism on our nation's campuses is rapidly becoming a national embarrassment. Almost daily, we are faced with headlines featuring some of the ugliest forms of ethnic conflict and the specter of virtually all-white universities. The need to avoid these consequences may have the beneficial effect of causing courts to reflect on, and tailor, constitutional doctrine. As Harry Kalven pointed out twenty-five years ago, it would not be the first time that insights born of the cauldron of racial justice yielded reforms that ultimately redounded to the benefit of all society.

We began by pointing out a little-noticed indeterminacy in the way campus anti-racism rules are analyzed. Such rules may be seen either as posing a First Amendment problem or falling within the ambit of the equality-protecting amendments. The survey of the experience of other nations in regulating hate speech and the writings of social scientists on race and racism do not dispel this indeterminacy. Each view is plausible; each corresponds to a deeply held narrative; each proceeds from one's life experiences; each is backed by constitutional case law and principle. Each lays claim to the higher education imperative that our campuses reflect a marketplace of ideas.

The gap between the two approaches can be addressed by means of a postmodern insight: racist speech is different because it is the means by which society constructs a stigma-picture of disfavored groups. It is tacitly coordinated by its speakers in a broad design, each act of which seems harmless but which, in combination with others, crushes the spirits of its victims while creating culture at odds with our national values. Only by taking account of this group dimension can we capture the full power of racially scathing speech—and make good on our promises of equal citizenship to those who have so long been denied its reality.

Parents Are Entitled to Ban Books

by D.J. Tice

About the author: *D.J. Tice is an editorial writer for the* Saint Paul Pioneer Press.

Toward the end of Mark Twain's *The Adventures of Huckleberry Finn,* Aunt Sally questions Huck about a recent steamboat trip.

"What's kep you?—boat get aground?"

"It weren't the grounding. We blowed out a cylinder head."

"Good gracious! Anybody hurt?"

"No'm. Killed a nigger."

"Well, it's lucky; because sometimes people do get hurt . . ."

The Fallacies of Banned Books Week

Happy Banned Books Week (September 28–October 4 [1997])—that whimsical event near the start of each school year when America's librarians imagine tyranny lurking wherever parents worry about the books their children are reading.

Each year for example, we're invited to suppose black parents are being ridiculous when they object to schools exposing their kids to *Huckleberry Finn*—perennially among the most frequently challenged books.

Well, they're not. *Huck Finn* is an exquisite work of art and a shattering protest against racism. But as the passage above suggests, it is also an acid satire that assuredly could scar an impressionable black child. Parents concerned about the novel's suitability for children deserve a respectful hearing. So do lots of other parents worried about other books.

Unfortunately, Banned Books Week suggests instead that parents are launching a repressive attack on free speech anytime they question the books their children are assigned, or find in school libraries. More than eight in ten of the "challenges" listed by the American Library Association for Banned Books

Week involve school books.

Most challenges fail. No doubt that's because most challenged books, like *Huck Finn*, have literary merit to compensate for their troubling social or sexual content.

Then again, the intellectual life of Gainesville, Georgia, has perhaps not been irretrievably dimmed by the loss of *Women on Top; How Real Life Has Changed Women's Fantasies*; this masterpiece's removal under protest from public library shelves is among the blows to human freedom being lamented this Banned Books Week.

To give credit where it's due, 1997's Banned Books Week press materials seem more moderate in tone than in years past. There's a constructive new recognition that parents challenging books are just trying to do their job as parents by monitoring what their children are reading.

But the underlying premise of Banned Books Week remains dubious. It contributes to Americans' continuing confusion and exasperation about the rights of free speech and free expression.

Rejection Is Not Censorship

Banned Books Week suggests that in order to honor free expression, Americans must never ask schools or libraries to uphold cultural and community standards. Parents must be left entirely on their own in protecting their children from offensive materials. Such extreme notions help lead to cynicism, and perversely, to impatience with freedom of free expression.

The U.S. Constitution and American tradition forbid the government from interfering with free expression, as in book publishing. But nothing in law or principle requires a school to use a book officials consider unworthy. Choices to use some books and reject others are made constantly, and parents are doing nothing wrong in trying to influence those choices.

> *"Parents challenging books are just trying to do their job as parents by monitoring what their children are reading."*

So long as a book's right to be published remains unthreatened, its rejection by a school or library is not "censorship." It is simply the "free expression" of a community's taste and morality.

Government Censorship Is Wrong

If the community's right to cultural self-defense were clearer to people, perhaps fewer Americans would be tempted to cross the line that must not be crossed by seeking government prohibition of unpopular messages.

Consider the Minnesota state law, struck down by the Court of Appeals, that tried to outlaw Crazy Horse Malt Liquor—a foolish and flagrant act of government censorship.

But notice, please, that bars and liquor stores and media companies are perfectly free to decline to sell or advertise such obnoxious products as Crazy Horse. It need not be served at the community picnic. Citizens groups are free to encourage its rejection.

As Indians feel about Crazy Horse brew, military veterans feel about a burning American flag. The anti-flag burning forces' campaign to outlaw disrespect for America is a betrayal of America's free tradition—though at least they're making a forthright effort to enact a constitutional amendment banning the expression they hate.

Less respect for the Constitution is evident in America's current president who has imposed by executive order sweeping prohibitions on cigarette advertising that are almost certainly unconstitutional.

But of course stores need not sell cigarettes, media firms need not accept cigarette advertising, and schools sure as sunrise need not stock reading materials that recommend cigarettes.

Nearly everyone, truth be told, finds it difficult to consistently support freedom of expression. It helps to know it's balanced against the freedom of individuals and communities to decline to pass on messages they disapprove.

Chapter 3

Should Pornography Be Censored?

Censoring Pornography: An Overview

by Fred H. Cate

About the author: *Fred H. Cate is a professor of law and director of the Information Law and Commerce Institute at the Indiana University School of Law—Bloomington.*

Despite the extraordinary breadth of the First Amendment, the Supreme Court has found that the amendment's protection does not extend to the distribution or public exhibition of sexually explicit expression that is "obscene." In 1957 in *Roth v. United States,* the Court held that "obscenity is not within the area of constitutionally protected speech or press." Although the Court declined to provide a specific definition for "obscenity," its analysis focused on whether the average person, applying contemporary community standards, would find that the dominant theme of the material taken as a whole appealed to "prurient" interests.

Roth set off more than a decade of judicial confusion and indecision about the definition of obscenity, leading the late Justice [Potter] Stewart to write in 1964 that an intelligent definition might be impossible, but "I know it when I see it." On 31 occasions, the Court reviewed purportedly obscene material and rendered a judgment as to its permissibility. Justice [William] Brennan complained that the examination of this material was "hardly a source of edification to the members of this Court . . . [and] has cast us in the role of an unreviewable board of censorship for the 50 states." In 1966, in a plurality opinion, the Court narrowed the definition of "obscenity" by requiring that lower courts find to be obscene only works that are *"utterly* without redeeming social value." Still, the definition of obscenity lacked the clarity needed to provide the meaningful guidance to citizens and local governments that ultimately would reduce the Court's role as a national board of censorship.

In 1973 the Court finally adopted a specific, albeit still subjective, definition of obscenity. In *Miller v. California,* a 5–4 majority held that works are obscene, and therefore outside the protection of the First Amendment, only if

Excerpted from Fred H. Cate, *The Internet and the First Amendment: Schools and Sexually Explicit Expression.* Reprinted with permission from Phi Delta Kappa Educational Foundation.

1) "the average person, applying contemporary community standards" would find that the work, taken as a whole, appeals to the prurient interest; 2) the work depicts or describes, in a patently offensive way, sexual or excretory conduct specifically defined by the applicable state law; and 3) the work, taken as a whole, lacks serious literary, artistic, political, or scientific value. The "prurient interest" requirement, the Court later ruled, is satisfied only by expression that does more than "provoke only normal, healthy sexual desires." In *Miller* and subsequent cases, the Court stressed that the first two prongs of the test could be judged under subjective local or state community standards. "People in different States vary in their tastes and attitudes, and this diversity is not to be strangled by the absolutism of imposed uniformity," Chief Justice [Warren] Burger wrote for the Court in *Miller.* There cannot be "fixed, uniform national standards of precisely what appeals to the 'prurient interest' or is 'patently offensive.'. . . [O]ur nation is simply too big and too diverse for this Court to reasonably expect that such standards could be articulated for all 50 states in a single formulation." Redeeming literary, artistic, political, or scientific value, on the other hand, is not a subject for local standards and must therefore be judged under a national "reasonable person" standard.

Contemporaneously with the *Roth-Miller* line of cases, which dealt with distributing and displaying publicly obscene material, the Court also decided *Stanley v. Georgia,* which involved the possession of obscenity. In *Stanley* the Court held, without dissent, that the Constitution protected the possession of sexually explicit material, even if it was legally obscene. While the "[s]tates retain broad power to regulate obscenity," Justice [Thurgood] Marshall wrote for the Court, "that power simply does not extend to mere possession by the individual in the privacy of his own home." The Court based its decision both on the "right to receive information and ideas, regardless of their social worth," which Justice Marshall wrote "is fundamental to our free society," and on the "right to be free, except in very limited circumstances, from unwanted governmental intrusion into one's privacy." Characterizing the Georgia law at issue in the case, which criminalized possession of obscene material, as a "drastic invasion of personal liberties guaranteed by the First and Fourteenth Amendments," the Court concluded: "If the First Amendment means anything, it means that a State has no business telling a man, sitting alone in his own house, what books he may read or

> *"The Supreme Court has found that the [First Amendment's] protection does not extend to the distribution or public exhibition of sexually explicit expression that is 'obscene.'"*

what films he may watch. Our whole constitutional heritage rebels at the thought of giving government the power to control men's minds."

While the *Miller* test failed to end the controversy over the definition of obscenity and has pleased few free speech advocates with its abandonment of

Roth's "utterly without redeeming social value" standard, it has emphasized the narrowness of the so-called "obscenity" exception to the First Amendment. When both the audience and the participants, if any, are consenting adults, the First Amendment protects all expression other than that meeting the *Miller* definition of obscenity. And the determination of whether specific expression fits within that definition requires that the state specifically define the conduct or expression to be prohibited; that the expression offend the standards of the local or, at most,

> *"When the . . . participants are not limited to consenting adults, courts have interpreted the First Amendment to permit greater regulation, . . . of sexually explicit expression."*

state community; and that the literary, artistic, political, or scientific value be judged according to a national, reasonable person standard. Expression not meeting the *Miller* definition, judged according to these procedural and substantive safeguards, is not obscene and is protected by the First Amendment. Such words and phrases as "pornography" or "lewd, lascivious, and filthy" or "XXX," which may be used to describe sexually explicit expression, have no legal significance. Expression that meets the *Miller* definition for obscenity may be prohibited only insofar as the regulation applies to distribution or public display. Under *Stanley,* the mere possession of obscenity is fully protected by the First Amendment.

Defining Obscenity

Miller has largely defined state obscenity law. Rather than merely mark the contours of acceptable obscenity regulation, as the Court anticipated, the case has been followed by virtually all states as articulating the definition of obscenity. Indiana state law, for example, defines obscenity as follows:

A matter or performance is obscene for purposes of this article if:

(1) The average person, applying contemporary community standards, finds that the dominant theme of the matter or performance, taken as a whole, appeals to the prurient interest in sex;

(2) The matter or performance depicts or describes, in a patently offensive way, sexual conduct; and

(3) The matter or performance, taken as a whole, lacks serious literary, artistic, political, or scientific value.

State law does not define "prurient interest in sex" or "serious literary, artistic, political, or scientific value."

Indiana state law prohibits the knowing or intentional importation, distribution, exhibition, or performance of obscene material:

A person who knowingly or intentionally:

(1) Sends or brings into Indiana obscene matter for sale or distribution; or

(2) Offers to distribute, distributes, or exhibits to another person obscene matter;

commits a Class A misdemeanor. However, the offense is a Class D felony if the obscene matter depicts or describes sexual conduct involving any person who is or appears to be under sixteen (16) years of age.

A person who knowingly or intentionally engages in, participates in, manages, produces, sponsors, presents, exhibits, photographs, films, or videotapes any obscene performance commits a Class A misdemeanor. However, the offense is a Class D felony if the obscene performance depicts or describes sexual conduct involving any person who is or appears to be under sixteen (16) years of age.

Read together, *Miller* and *Stanley* indicate that it is only the threat of possible harm posed by distribution or public performance of obscene material, and not posed by its possession, that permits the criminalization of the former but not the latter. The Court's logic therefore suggests that if it were possible to receive obscenity in the home without posing any of the risks that distribution or public performance were feared inherently to impose—for example, exposure to minors, accidental exposure to unwitting adults, and such "secondary" effects as prostitution and neighborhood deterioration—then the First Amendment would require that the government permit it. In fact, the Court went out of its way in *Stanley* to note that even if it could be shown "that exposure to obscene materials may lead to deviant sexual behavior or crimes of sexual violence"—an assertion for which the Court found "little empirical basis"—"the State may no more prohibit mere possession of obscene matter on the ground that it may lead to anti-social conduct than it may prohibit possession of chemistry books on the ground that they may lead to the manufacture of homemade spirits."

In practice, state law enforcement officials exploit the subjective nature of the first two parts of the *Miller* test, the high cost of litigation, and the political visibility of anti-porn "crackdowns" to effectively threaten many distributors of sexually explicit images and videos. (Suits for text-based obscenity alone are rare.) Defendants often settle rather than endure the tactics of government officials, the cost of a trial, the negative publicity associated with being tried and arrested, and the risk of a conviction. Nonetheless, it is still clear that the law protects a very broad range of sexually explicit expression.

Limiting Minors' Access to Pornography

When the audience or participants are not limited to consenting adults, courts have interpreted the First Amendment to permit greater regulation, or even prohibition, of sexually explicit expression. This is particularly true when children are involved. For example, the Supreme Court has found that states not only may criminalize the depiction of children in sexually explicit films and photographs, they also may prohibit the distribution and even the mere possession of those films and photographs in an effort to eliminate the market for child pornography.

The government also may constitutionally require suppliers of sexually explicit expression to restrict children's access to that expression. Sometimes referred to as "variable obscenity," this concept permits states to require sellers of non-obscene, "adult" books, magazines, and videos to stock those items in a section of the store inaccessible to children, to display them with opaque wrappers, or to require proof of age from people entering "adult" book and video stores. Indiana, for example, typical of many states, designates some material or performances as "harmful to minors" if:

> *"Material that is not obscene for adults nonetheless may be harmful to children."*

1) It describes or represents, in any form, nudity, sexual conduct, sexual excitement, or sado-masochistic abuse;

2) Considered as a whole, it appeals to the prurient interest in sex of minors;

3) It is patently offensive to prevailing standards in the adult community as a whole with respect to what is suitable matter for or performance before minors; and

4) Considered as a whole, it lacks serious literary, artistic, political, or scientific value for minors.

State law broadly prohibits making such material or performances available to minors.

A person who knowingly or intentionally:

1) Disseminates matter to minors that is harmful to minors;

2) Displays matter that is harmful to minors in an area to which minors have visual, auditory, or physical access, unless each minor is accompanied by his parent or guardian;

3) Sells or displays for sale to any person matter that is harmful to minors within five hundred feet (500') of the nearest property line of a school or church;

4) Engages in or conducts a performance before minors that is harmful to minors;

5) Engages in or conducts a performance that is harmful to minors in an area to which minors have visual, auditory, or physical access, unless each minor is accompanied by his parent or guardian; . . .

commits a Class D felony.

Cannot Limit Adults' Rights

Laws such as this recognize that material that is not obscene for adults nonetheless may be harmful to children. Interestingly, neither legislatures nor courts have sought to identify precisely the risk such material poses to children. Because protecting children is a compelling state interest, courts simply have deferred to legislative determinations that accessing sexually explicit material does in fact harm children. Legislators, in turn, have largely assumed that such harm exists. It is beyond the purview of this viewpoint to debate the existence of such harm, but it is sufficient to note that legislatures and courts alike have based a great deal of jurisprudence on the *assumption* that exposure to sexually explicit material does harm children. And courts have therefore permitted extensive regulation of children's access to sexually explicit material. The constitutional limit on those restrictions, according to the Supreme Court, is that they must not limit what adults may read to "only what is fit for children." "Regardless of the strength of the government's interest" in protecting children, the Court has written, "the level of discourse reaching the mailbox simply cannot be limited to that which would be suitable for a sandbox." The Court's most recent cases indicate that no incursion into the First Amendment rights of adults is permissible in order to protect children if it is not necessary and effective as a means of controlling minors' access.

Pornography Should Be Censored

by Irving Kristol

About the author: *Irving Kristol is the editor of the* Public Interest *and the publisher of the* National Interest.

Pornography differs from erotic art in that its whole purpose is to treat human beings obscenely, to deprive human beings of their specifically human dimension. That is what obscenity is all about. It is light-years removed from any kind of carefree sensuality—there is no continuum between Fielding's *Tom Jones* and the Marquis de Sade's *Justine.* These works have quite opposite intentions. To quote Susan Sontag: "What pornographic literature does is precisely to drive a wedge between one's existence as a full human being and one's existence as a sexual being—while in ordinary life a healthy person is one who prevents such a gap from opening up." This definition occurs in an essay *defending* pornography—Miss Sontag is a candid as well as gifted critic—so the definition, which I accept, is neither tendentious nor censorious.

Language and Mores

Along these same lines, one can point out—as C.S. Lewis pointed out some years back—that it is no accident that in the history of all literatures, obscene words, the so-called four-letter words, have always been the vocabulary of farce or vituperation. The reason is clear; they reduce men and women to some of their mere bodily functions—they reduce man to his animal component, and such a reduction is an essential purpose of farce or vituperation.

Similarly, Lewis also suggested that it is not an accident that we have no off-hand, colloquial, neutral terms—not in any Western European language at any rate—for our most private parts. The words we do use are either (1) nursery terms, (2) archaisms, (3) scientific terms, or (4) a term from the gutter (i.e., a demeaning term). Here I think the genius of language is telling us something important about man. It is telling us that man is an animal with a difference: He has a unique sense of privacy, and a unique capacity for shame when this privacy is violated. Our "private parts" are indeed private, and not merely because convention prescribes it. This particular convention is indigenous to the human race. In practically all primitive tribes, men and women cover their private parts; and in practically all primitive tribes, men and women do not copulate in public.

It may well be that Western society, in the latter half of the twentieth century, is experiencing a drastic change in sexual mores and sexual relationships. We have had many such "sexual revolutions" in the past—the bourgeois family and bourgeois ideas of sexual propriety were themselves established in the course of a revolution against eighteenth-century "licentiousness"—and we shall doubtless have others in the future. It is, however, highly improbable (to put it mildly) that what we are witnessing is the Final Revolution which will make sexual relations utterly unproblematic, permit us to dispense with any kind of ordered relationships between the sexes, and allow us freely to redefine the human condition. And so long as humanity has not reached that utopia, obscenity will remain a problem.

Inappropriate Public Spectacles

Imagine a man—a well-known man, much in the public eye—in a hospital ward, dying an agonizing death. He is not in control of his bodily functions, so that his bladder and his bowels empty themselves of their own accord. His consciousness is overwhelmed and extinguished by pain, so that he cannot communicate with us, nor we with him. Now, it would be, technically, the easiest thing in the world to put a television camera in his hospital room and let the whole world witness this spectacle. We do not do it—at least we do not do it as yet—because we regard this as an *obscene* invasion of privacy. And what would make the spectacle obscene is that we would be witnessing the extinguishing of humanity in a human animal.

Incidentally, in the past our humanitarian crusaders against capital punishment understood this point very well. The abolitionist literature goes into great physical detail about what happens to a man when he is hanged or electrocuted or gassed. Their argument was—and is—that what happens is shockingly obscene, and that no civilized society should be responsible for perpetrating such obscenities, particularly since in the nature of the case there must be spectators to ascertain this horror was indeed being perpetrated in fulfillment of the law.

> *"When sex is a public spectacle, a human relationship has been debased into a mere animal connection."*

Sex—like death—is an activity that is both animal and human. There are human sentiments and human ideals involved in this animal activity. But when sex is public, the viewer does not see—cannot see—the sentiments and the ideals. He can only see the animal coupling. And that is why, when men and women make love, as we say, they prefer to be alone—because it is only when you are alone that you can make love, distinct from merely copulating in an animal and casual way. And that, too, is why those who are voyeurs, if they are not irredeemably sick, also feel ashamed at what they are witnessing. When sex is a public spectacle, a human relationship has been debased into a mere animal connection.

It is also worth noting that this making of sex into an obscenity is not a mutual and equal transaction but rather an act of exploitation by one of the partners—the male partner. I do not wish to get into the complicated question as to what, if any, are the essential differences—as distinct from conventional and cultural differences—between male and female. I do not claim to know the answer to that. But I do know—and I take it as a sign that has meaning—that pornography is, and always has been, a man's work; that women rarely write pornography. There are of course, a few exceptions. *L'Historie d'O*, for example, was written by a woman. It is unquestionably the most *melancholy* work of pornography ever written. And its theme is precisely the dehumanization accomplished by obscenity.

My own guess, by way of explanation, is that a woman's sexual experience is ordinarily more suffused with human emotion than is a man's, that men are more easily satisfied with autoerotic activities, and that men can therefore more easily take a more "technocratic" view of sex and its pleasures. Perhaps this is not correct. But whatever the explanation, there can be no question that pornography is a form of "sexism," as the women's liberation movement calls it, and that the instinct of women's liberation has been unerring in perceiving that when pornography is perpetrated, it is perpetrated against them, as part of a conspiracy to deprive them of their full humanity.

> *"The basic psychological fact about pornography . . . is that it appeals to and provokes a kind of sexual regression."*

Arguments Against Pornography

But even if all this is granted, it might be said—and doubtless will be said—that I really ought not to be unduly concerned. Free competition in the cultural marketplace—it is argued by people who have never otherwise had a kind word to say for laissez-faire—will automatically dispose of the problem. The present fad for pornography and obscenity, it will be asserted, is just that, a fad. It will spend itself in the course of time; people will get bored with it, will be able to take it or leave it alone in a casual way, in a "mature way" and, in sum, I am being unnecessarily distressed about the whole business.

I would like to be able to go along with this line of reasoning, but I cannot. I think it is false, and for two reasons, the first psychological, the second political.

The basic psychological fact about pornography and obscenity is that it appeals to and provokes a kind of sexual regression. The sexual pleasure one gets from pornography and obscenity is autoerotic and infantile; put bluntly, it is a masturbatory exercise of the imagination, when it is not masturbation pure and simple. Now, people who masturbate do not get bored with masturbation, just as sadists do not get bored with sadism, and voyeurs do not get bored with voyeurism.

In other words, infantile sexuality is not only a permanent temptation for the adolescent or even the adult—it can quite easily become a permanent, self-reinforcing neurosis. It is

> *"The matter of pornography and obscenity is not a trivial one, and only superficial minds can take a bland and untroubled view of it."*

because of an awareness of this possibility of regression toward the infantile condition, a regression which is not always open to us, that all the codes of sexual conduct ever devised by the human race take such a dim view of autoerotic activities and try to discourage autoerotic fantasies. Masturbation is indeed a perfectly natural autoerotic activity, as so many sexologists blandly assure us today. And it is precisely because it is so perfectly natural that it can be so dangerous to the mature or maturing person, if it is not controlled or sublimated in some way. That is the true meaning of Portnoy's complaint. [*Portnoy's Complaint* is a book by Philip Roth.] Portnoy, you will recall, grows up to be a man who is incapable of having an adult sexual relationship with a woman; his sexuality remains fixed in an infantile mode, the prisoner of his autoerotic fantasies. Inevitably, Portnoy comes to think, in a perfectly *infantile* way, that it was all his mother's fault.

Civilization Is at Stake

It is true that, in our time, some quite brilliant minds have come to the conclusion that a reversion to infantile sexuality is the ultimate mission and secret destiny of the human race. I am thinking in particular of Norman O. Brown, for whose writings I have the deepest respect. One of the reasons I respect them so deeply is that Mr. Brown is a serious thinker who is unafraid to face up to the radical consequences of his radical theories. Thus, Mr. Brown knows and says that for his kind of salvation to be achieved, humanity must annul the civilization it has created—not merely the civilization we have today, but all civilization—so as to be able to make the long descent backward into animal innocence.

And that is the point. What is at stake is civilization and humanity, nothing less. The idea that "everything is permitted," as [German philosopher] Nietzsche put it, rests or the premise of nihilism and has nihilistic implications. I will not pretend that the case against nihilism and for civilization is an easy one to make. We are here confronting the most fundamental of philosophical questions, on the deepest levels. In short, the matter of pornography and obscenity is not a trivial one, and only superficial minds can take a bland and untroubled view of it.

In this connection, I must point out, those who are primarily against censorship on liberal grounds tell us not to take pornography or obscenity seriously, while those who are for pornography and obscenity on radical grounds take it very seriously indeed. I believe radicals—writers like Susan Sontag, Herbert Marcuse, Norman O. Brown, and even Jerry Rubin—are right, and the liberals are wrong. . . .

Why Pornography Must Be Censored

I have, it may be noticed, uttered that dreadful word censorship. And I am not about to back away from it. If you think pornography and/or obscenity is a serious problem, you have to be for censorship. I will go even further and say that if you want to prevent pornography and/or obscenity from becoming a problem, you have to be for censorship. And lest there be any misunderstanding as to what I am saying, I will put it as bluntly as possible: If you care for the quality of life in our American democracy, then you have to be for censorship.

But can a liberal be for censorship? Unless one assumes that being liberal *must* mean being indifferent to the quality of American life, then the answer has to be yes, a liberal can be for censorship—but he ought to favor a liberal form of censorship.

Is that a contradiction in terms? I do not think so. We have no problem in contrasting *repressive* laws governing alcohol and drugs and tobacco with laws *regulating* (i.e., discouraging the sale of) alcohol and drugs and tobacco. Laws encouraging temperance are not the same thing as laws that have as their goal prohibition or abolition. We have not made the smoking of cigarettes a criminal offense. We have, however, and with good liberal conscience, prohibited cigarette advertising on television, and may yet, again, with good liberal conscience, prohibit it in newspapers and magazines. The idea of restricting individual freedom in a liberal way, is not all unfamiliar to us.

I therefore see no reason why we should not be able to distinguish repressive censorship from liberal censorship of the written and spoken word. In Britain, until a few years ago, you could perform almost any play you wished, but certain plays, judged to be obscene, had to be performed in private theatrical clubs, which were deemed to have a "serious" interest in theatre.

> *"If you think pornography and/or obscenity is a serious problem, you have to be for censorship."*

In the United States, all of us who grew up using public libraries are familiar with the circumstances under which certain books could be circulated only to adults, while still other books had to be read in the library reading room, under the librarian's skeptical eye. In both cases, a small minority that was willing to make a serious effort to see an obscene play or read an obscene book could do so. But the impact of the obscenity was circumscribed and the quality of public life was only marginally affected.

Possible Problems with Liberal Censorship

It is fairly predictable that someone is going to object that this point of view is "elitist"—that, under a system of liberal censorship, the rich will have privileged access to pornography and obscenity. Yes, of course, they will—just as, at present, the rich have privileged access to heroin if they want it. But one would have to be an egalitarian maniac to object to this state of affairs on the grounds of equality.

I am not saying it is easy in practice to sustain a distinction between liberal and repressive censorship, especially in the public realm of democracy, where popular opinion is so vulnerable to demagoguery. Moreover, an acceptable system of liberal censorship is likely to be exceedingly difficult to devise in the United States today, because our educated classes, upon whose judgment a liberal censorship must rest, are so convinced that there is no such thing as obscenity at all. But to counterbalance this, there is the further, fortunate truth that the tolerable margin for error is quite large, and single mistakes or single injustices are not all that important.

This possibility of error, of course, occasions much distress among artists and academics. It is a fact, one that cannot and should not be denied, that any system of censorship is bound, upon occasion, to treat unjustly a particular work of art—to find pornography where there is only gentle eroticism, to find obscenity where none really exists, or to find both where its existence ought to be tolerated because it serves a larger moral purpose. Though most works of art are not obscene, and though most obscenity has nothing to do with art, there are some few works of art that are, at least in part, pornographic and/or obscene. There are also some few works of art that are in a special category of the comic-ironic "bawdy" (Boccaccio, Rabelais). It is such works of art that are likely to suffer at the hands of the censor. That is the price one has to be prepared to pay for censorship—even liberal censorship.

> *"Though most works of art are not obscene, and though most obscenity has nothing to do with art, there are some few works of art that are, at least in part, pornographic and/or obscene."*

Censorship Is Not Damaging

But just how high is this price? If you believe, as so many artists seem to believe today, that art is the only sacrosanct activity in our profane and vulgar world—that any man who designates himself an artist thereby acquires a sacred office—then obviously censorship is an intolerable form of sacrilege. But for those of us who do not subscribe to this religion of art, the costs of censorship do not seem high at all.

If you look at the history of American or English literature, there is precious little damage you can point to as a consequence of the censorship that prevailed throughout most of that history. Very few works of literature—of real literary merit, I mean—ever were suppressed; and those that were, were not suppressed for long. Nor have I noticed, now that censorship of the written word has to all intents and purposes ceased in this country, that the hitherto suppressed or repressed masterpieces are flooding the market. Yes, we can now read *Fanny Hill* and the Marquis de Sade. Or, to be more exact, we can now openly purchase them, since many people were able to read them even though they were publicly banned, which is as it should be under a liberal censorship. So how much have literature and the arts gained from the fact that we can all now buy them over the counter, that, indeed we are all now encouraged to buy them over the counter? They have not gained much that I can see.

> "I think the settlement we are living under now, in which obscenity and democracy are regarded as equals, is wrong."

And one might also ask the question that is almost never raised: How much has literature lost from the fact that everything is now permitted? It has lost quite a bit, I should say. In a free market, Gresham's Law [the economic principle that bad money drives out good] can work for books or theater as efficiently as it does for coinage—driving out the good, establishing the debased. The cultural market in the United States today is being preempted by dirty books, dirty movies, dirty theater. A pornographic novel has a far better chance of being published today than a non-pornographic one, and quite a few pretty good novels are not being published at all simply because they are not pornographic, and are therefore less likely to sell. Our cultural condition has not improved as a result of the new freedom. American cultural life was not much to brag about twenty years ago; today one feels ashamed for it.

Just one last point, which I dare not leave untouched. If we start censoring pornography and obscenity, shall we not inevitably end up censoring political opinion? A lot of people seem to think this would be the case—which only shows the power of doctrinaire thinking over reality. We had censorship of pornography and obscenity for 150 years, until almost yesterday, and I am not aware that freedom of opinion in this country was in any way diminished as a consequence of this fact. Fortunately for those of us who are liberal, freedom is not indivisible. If it were, the case for liberalism would be indistinguishable from the case for anarchy; and they are two very different things.

Obscenity Is Not Equal to Democracy

But I must repeat and emphasize: What kinds of laws we pass governing pornography and obscenity, what kind of censorship—or, since we are still a federal nation, what kinds of censorship—we institute in our various localities may indeed be difficult matters to cope with; nevertheless the real issue is one of principle. I myself subscribe to a liberal view of the enforcement problem: I think that pornography should be illegal *and* available to anyone who wants it so badly as to make a pretty strenuous effort to get it. We have lived with under-the-counter pornography for centuries now, in a fairly comfortable way. But the issue of principle, of whether it should be over or under the counter, has to be settled before we can reflect on the advantages and disadvantages of alternative modes of censorship. I think the settlement we are living under now, in which obscenity and democracy are regarded as equals, is wrong; I believe it is inherently unstable. I think it will in the long run, be incompatible with any authentic concern for the quality of life in our democracy.

Internet Filters Should Be Used to Reduce Access to Pornography

by Robert Marshall

About the author: *Robert Marshall is a member of the Virginia House of Delegates.*

A classroom or library with a computer and a modem hookup to the Internet is simply the latest in a long line of tools that aid information presentation and retrieval. In its functions, an Internet-linked computer is a combination of the following: a television, a radio, an electric typewriter, an electronic stenographer, an electronic Polaroid camera, a message service, a teletype, an electronic community bulletin board, an amateur or "ham" two-way radio, and a television station for camera-equipped computers or a local access long-distance phone (with echoes) for phone-equipped computers.

This combination of equipment doesn't produce magic boxes that mutate nature, amend the U.S. Constitution, or alter any of the Ten Commandments. Yet, when otherwise intelligent people approach Internet-linked computers, an attitude of untouchable reverence and unthinking acceptance overtakes even the likes of Supreme Court judges who pronounce that no human hand may interfere with the carnal electronic commerce of the Internet.

The illusion of Utopias has captured the human imagination whenever new frontiers are reached. Eventually, however, the realities of range wars and rustlers, bandits, badmen, brigands and roving outlaw gangs punctures the euphoria of even the hardiest pioneers. Those who opt for peace eventually accept restraints. Experience suggests the same conclusions will hold for those who now envision a boundless and conflict-free cyberspace.

In a case where state inmates were held to have a right to access a prison law library as a means to secure their civil and due process rights, the Supreme Court held that:

> Because *Bounds* [a previous case] did not create an abstract, free-standing right to a law library or legal assistance, an inmate cannot establish relevant actual injury simply by establishing that his prison's law library or legal assistance program is subpar in some theoretical sense. . . . This Court does not feel inmates need the entire U.S. Code Annotated. Most of that code deals with federal laws and regulations that would never involve a state prisoner. . . . In other words, *Bounds* does not guarantee inmates the wherewithal to transform themselves into litigating engines capable of filing everything from shareholder derivative actions to slip-and-fall claims.

If persons seeking to restore their liberty do not have a right to unlimited public subsidized research resources, how is it to be claimed that those who merely want to satisfy personal curiosity or secure information faster have a constitutional right to unlimited Internet access at public expense?

When a New York school board removed certain books from a public school library, certain parents (respondents) sued. The Supreme Court [in the 1982 case, *Board of Education v. Pico*] acknowledged that certain classes of books could be removed from a school library even if they were already part of an established collection:

> [R]espondents implicitly concede that an unconstitutional motivation would not be demonstrated if it were shown that petitioners [School Board] had decided to remove the books at issue because those books were pervasively vulgar. . . . And again, respondents concede that if it were demonstrated that the removal decision was based solely upon the 'educational suitability' of the books in question, then their removal would be 'perfectly permissible.'. . . [I]n respondents' view such motivations, if decisive of petitioners' actions, would not carry the danger of an official suppression of ideas, and thus would not violate respondents' First Amendment rights. . . . Nothing in our decision today affects in any way the discretion of a local school board to choose books to add to the libraries of their schools. . . .

The American Civil Liberties Union (ACLU) and American Library Association (ALA) claim that the *Pico* decision prevents a library from using an Internet filter on the grounds that it is equivalent to removing a book from a collection because of the viewpoint of the authors. However, in the real world, school and library boards of necessity select from the entire field of possible hard copy books and magazines to purchase and approve only certain ones. A filter that screens sexually explicit material is simply a tool that implements the normal selection and acquisition process.

Acting as Parents

Second, the number of Internet computer links from school and public libraries will of necessity be fewer than the number of potential patrons or students seeking Internet access. There will have to be some time and place restrictions on access to these information retrieval stations. Third, using a filter does not remove an "electronic" or virtual book, article, magazine or picture from a library because it was never there in the first place; it may only be temporarily retrieved. Interlibrary loans provide for temporary use by a patron library books not in the permanent collection of a library. Fourth, major Internet providers such as America Online and Walt Disney have agreed to provide parents with the tools to screen objectionable material. Because parents regularly delegate their direct supervisorial authority over their children to teachers and librarians who act *in loco parentis,* this fact significantly weakens ALA's opposition to school or library use of filters.

> *"A filter that screens sexually explicit material is simply a tool that implements the normal selection and acquisition process."*

For example, no school or library would insist that it were devoid of responsibility to act *in loco parentis* if a staff member left a bottle of toxic cleaning solution in a soda drink can on a table in the children's book corner. A different standard for children in the realm of physical negligence is justified in the same way a "harmful to minors" standard is in the realm of moral negligence.

Libraries Are Meant to Inform

The *Pico* decision held:

> [N]othing in our decision today affects in any way the discretion of a local school board to choose books to add to the libraries of their schools. Because we are concerned in this case with the suppression of ideas, our holding [457 U.S. 853, 872] today affects only the discretion to remove books. In brief, we hold that local school boards may not remove books from school library shelves simply because they dislike the ideas contained in those books and seek by their removal to 'prescribe what shall be orthodox in politics, nationalism, religion, or other matters of opinion.' *West Virginia Board of Education v. Barnette,* 319 U.S., at 642. Such purposes stand inescapably condemned by our precedents.

Thus, if a school or public library does not make available to students or patrons hard copies of *Hustler, Playboy* or Triple X books or videos, why must it make available digital or electronic versions of these same materials that do not meet the library's hard copy selection criteria? To suggest otherwise is to suggest that the Internet is a magic box utterly free from conventional and legal restraints routinely applied to other media.

Furthermore, the Supreme Court elsewhere has held: "A school library, no less than any other public library, is 'a place dedicated to quiet, to knowledge, and to beauty.'" Turning a library over to community "shock jocks," pedophiles and pornographers would, because of the social disruption caused by leaving public displays of objectionable sexual material on library computers, turn the library from its basic mission, which is to inform citizens, not to sensually arouse them.

Internet Filters Do Not Violate the First Amendment

The ACLU, ALA, and other plaintiffs did not challenge in *ACLU v. Reno* a provision of the Communications Decency Act of 1996 that specifically authorizes Internet providers, including state and local governments with respect to public libraries and schools, to be immune from liability for screening certain material. The decision of the Court in *ACLU v. Reno* left this provision intact. The CDA provision states:

> No provider or user of an interactive service shall be held liable on account of (A) any action voluntarily taken in good faith to restrict access to or availability of material that the provider or user considers to be obscene, lewd, lascivious, filthy, excessively violent, harassing, or otherwise objectionable, whether or not such material is constitutionally protected; or (B) any action taken to enable or make available to information content providers or others the technical means to restrict access to material. . . .

Such restrictions can include library employees' monitoring of public usage of computers, the placement of computers in a library, honor codes, time limits, the ability to print or save material as a computer file, the installation and use of Internet filters to screen disruptive material, and so on.

Pornography and Sexual Harassment

Public displays of pornography or other sexually suggestive material can create an uncomfortable and humiliating environment for persons exposed to them, whether in the workplace or in schools and libraries. This is legally termed sexual harassment.

Where students or library patrons leave sexually suggestive material on computer screens, especially that considered harmful to minors under state laws, and other students or library patrons who object to such material encounter the displays, the school administration has a legal responsibility to prevent such harassment from taking place in the future. Where a school district fails to do so, it would be subject to sexual harassment suits, with payouts coming from taxpayer funds to those offended by such displays.

> *"Using a filter does not remove an 'electronic' or virtual book, article, magazine, or picture from a library because it was never there in the first place."*

The U.S. Congress and federal courts have applied education-related civil rights laws against sexual discrimination to instances of "harassment" where a hostile environment pervades a workplace or an educational institution. Thus, a public school may be responsible for the acts of its employees who are in authority over students, and for the acts of students who sexually harass other students where the school knows or should have known of the problem but fails to take immediate and appropriate corrective action.

Along these lines, Attorney General Edwin Meese's Pornography Commission concluded in 1986:

> All institutions which are taxpayer funded should prohibit the production, trafficking, distribution, or display of pornography on their premises or in association with their institution to the extent constitutionally permissible. . . . [S]chools are the most obvious example. Content-based restrictions of the material available in the institution need not be restricted to the legally obscene, and we recognize not only the right but the responsibility of such institutions to control content consistent with the needs of the institution. . . .

Choosing Resources

In advocating a completely unregulated regimen of patron access to public computer equipment, the ACLU and ALA are proposing practices that are not followed anywhere else in library systems. For example, librarians will not choose one book on the Civil War by a scholar and another by a dunce for "balance" or fall prey to a claim that purchasing one and not the other violates a patron's First Amendment rights. Yet, the scholar and the dunce both have equal access to publish web pages on the Internet that will be retrieved by search queries on Internet browsers. A good publisher will accept the one and reject the other, but not the Internet.

Moreover, why should the library's Internet computer be just for academic research? Don't citizens have a right to play games all afternoon? What if some patrons want to add their own software to the library computer? Does preventing them from doing so deny any First Amendment freedom of expression? Hardly. If a library doesn't provide patrons free phones or mailing services, is refusal to provide patrons live "chat" rooms or e-mail a violation of the First Amendment? No, but that is where the ACLU's arguments logically lead.

It is the prime function of a librarian or library board to evaluate competing claims for library resources, with the result that some materials are chosen and others are not. The resources of a particular Internet service provider (ISP) are not infinite. Just like phone lines that are used to make the Internet connections, an ISP's system can slow down response time or even shut down because of an overload of pornographic traffic. The University of Virginia experienced this when an undetermined number of Internet users were trying to access the pornographic web page of a UVA student a couple of years ago.

Picking and choosing books and other resources is not a First Amendment problem for librarians if it is done on the basis of content, and not the author's viewpoint. Confusion here is counted on by the ACLU and the ALA to overwhelm public opposition to unfiltered or unregulated Internet access at public libraries.

The ACLU and ALA's arguments are addressed by Bruce Taylor and Bob Flores of the National Legal Center, a research organization that fights pornographers.

How to Combat Internet Pornography

There are proper roles for federal and state laws in the effort to keep the Internet safe for children.

The following suggestions should be incorporated into any state laws governing direct Internet access by students or library patrons in your state's public schools and libraries. Unfortunately, no real widespread informed debate has taken place in America concerning the utility of computers in the learning process, and more specifically the adaptability of the Internet, whether regulated or not, to the educational mission and function of the classroom and school library. Nevertheless, computers are being installed, and Congress has made available more than $2 billion dollars to get all the nation's public schools wired for the Internet.

The general conditions of Internet use in schools and public libraries that lawmakers should try to establish are as follows:

• No school computer in a classroom, lab, or library used by a student may be used to access material that is harmful to minors.

• For students in the eighth grade and under, all websites must be preapproved by the Superintendent of the Division as suitable for educational purposes.

• Because sexual predators try to contact children anonymously to gain the confidence of children as a prelude to sexual exploitation, on any school system offering e-mail to students 17 and under, e-mail contact with students should be limited (a) only to those persons authorized by the parents of the student, or (b) to other students within the school system.

• No computer in a school division accessed by students, school personnel or other authorized users may be used in a manner that would constitute sexual harassment of students, teachers, or other school personnel, or that would create a hostile work environment. There should be a rebuttable presumption for civil litigation purposes that the use of a school computer has caused a hostile work environment when such system has been used to access material that a reasonable person would find lewd, lascivious or sexually arousing.

> *"Picking and choosing books and other resources is not a First Amendment problem for librarians if it is done on the basis of content."*

• Students who use computers should be under adult supervision at all times. The normal standard of custodial care in a public institution due to minors may not be abrogated.

• Parents should have to sign an informed consent form in their own native language and with the risks explained in terms that would be understood by one who is not familiar with the operation of computers.

The Role of Library Boards

A library board should develop guidelines to apply the criteria it uses to serve its patron community for selecting books and other materials to site selection on the Internet. If you have it on the shelf, you can have it on the Internet—including *Gray's Anatomy,* books about AIDS prevention, etc.

Because of the ease with which such material can be accessed via the Internet without even seeking it, for adult computers the Library Board (Trustees) should develop and implement guidelines on the use of computer technology or software that would prevent accessing Internet material that is obscene or pornographic. Specifically, library boards of trustees should develop and implement guidelines for accessing material from the Internet by the use of computer hardware or software in a way not inconsistent with the library's selection policy or practice for its collection, which would prevent or which is designed to prevent the accession of Internet material that depicts: (a) the lewd or lascivious exhibition of genitals; (b) adults engaged in intercourse, masturbation or simulated masturbation; (c) sexual acts where penetration is clearly visible; (d) sexual acts between humans and animals; (e) bondage or sadomasochistic abuse; (f) ultimate sexual acts; (g) minors engaged in sexual acts; (h) coprophilia or urophilia; or (i) other sexual or excretory acts as defined and prohibited in the state criminal code.

> *"There are proper roles for federal and state laws in the effort to keep the Internet safe for children."*

Also, there should be a findings section of both the school and public library bill that would in effect spell out legislative intent for the inevitable federal judge who will try to find reasons for invalidating such statutes. If the purpose and/or findings of the law are spelled out in the law itself, federal judges will not be so easily able to substitute their own legislative intent for that of the state legislature. Furthermore, they will not easily be able to claim that legislators did not know what they were voting for, or that they really did not understand its effects.

A Suggested Statute

Thus, the statute should acknowledge the following "findings" for the school and public library as they may apply in their respective contexts:

1. It is the purpose of the legislature to provide an opportunity for educational advancement for all students in a manner that is compatible with their social well-being;

2. In exercising content selection of material that is educationally appropriate, there must be no effort to discriminate on the basis of viewpoint (in the case of adults using public libraries, the selection policy or practice for electronic collections should be the same selection policy or practice that prevails for hard copy collections of books, articles, magazines, etc.);

3. The legislature of (insert your state) notes that the use of pornography is predominantly a preoccupation of some males, and that young girls (women for public libraries) are subject to sexual harassment using sexually oriented pictures and text;

4. The legislature of (insert your state) finds that the accessing of pornography by the use of government-owned or government-leased classroom computers may inhibit adolescent females from choosing the best paying career opportunities (or achieving their educational goals);

5. The law should cite the federal Communications Decency Act which allows for restriction of even constitutionally protected material from the Internet;

6. There should be a recognition that public property must be used for the common good and for its intended purposes, and that other state property is not allowed to be used to harass citizens;

> *"A library board should develop guidelines to apply the criteria it uses to serve its patron community for selecting books . . . to site selection on the Internet."*

7. The constitution or laws of (insert your state) places an obligation on conservators of public property to ensure that, like other state property used for communication or information retrieval purposes, government-owned computers are not used for illegal purposes, including but not limited to retrieving, storing or displaying obscenity, child pornography, or perpetrating copyright violations; the destruction of the property via computer viruses; stealing money; or gaining illegal access to state or private records, all of which the legislature finds is prevalent on the Internet.

8. Furthermore, Internet access via state- or local jurisdiction-owned computers does not abolish the police powers of (insert your state) or its subsidiaries (counties, cities and towns), and information retrieval over the Information Infrastructure is simply using public property as part of a limited public forum which it may or may not provide.

9. Teachers, librarians and other school personnel with supervisory capacity over computers are obligated to monitor improper or illegal use of school computers and report violations to the proper school or legal authorities.

Additional Requirements

There should be an enhanced penalty for violations of this law because (a) familiarity with computers is becoming more and more a part of the formal learning process; (b) there is a generational gap between children and parents regarding how to use computers; and (c) the state has an obligation to provide a learning environment for children. (Schools are drug-free zones and have heightened penalties for drug pushers, or those who use guns illegally near schools.)

Additional requirements for public libraries that provide direct patron Internet access:

1. Apply the harmful to minors and sexual harassment or hostile workplace requirements to public libraries.

2. If more than one terminal in the library is dedicated to direct patron access, then the library must set aside a separate computer(s) for minors in a separate area within the library.

The statute should also stipulate that any public library or school has the authority to be more restrictive in its regulations or policies that are not in conflict with these state laws.

Sexual Material Is Too Widely Censored

by Marilyn C. Mazur and Joan E. Bertin

About the authors: Marilyn C. Mazur is an attorney for the National Coalition Against Censorship. Joan E. Bertin is the executive director of the NCAC.

> *We are working up a fever making new laws against touching, and we're more scandalized by a photograph or painting showing a nipple or a penis than by the image of a starving child on a dry, dusty road.*
>
> Thomas Moore, *Mother Jones*,
> September/October 1997

> *It's Sodom and Gomorrah all over again.*
>
> Dr. Robert L. Simonds,
> Citizens for Excellence in Education

Are Jock Sturges' photographs of nude children on the beach child pornography? Does learning about sex or reading about homosexuality cause young people to experiment with sex in ways they otherwise wouldn't? Should children be shielded from nudity in art and sex on the Internet? Can words like "masturbation" and "contraception" be banned from classroom discussions? Should parents always have the final say about what minors can read, see, and learn?

Sex and Minors

These are the issues at the center of many of the censorship wars in late 20th century America. In one sense, it's part of our tradition. From the ban on Margaret Sanger's use of the words syphilis and gonorrhea to the ban on James Joyce and Henry Miller, the censors have traditionally focused on sex. The debate has shifted, however. While First Amendment protection now extends to a great deal of material with sexual content—at least for adults—where children are concerned, all bets are off. As a result, most censorship wars over sex are now fought ostensibly to protect minors, and to define what is "harmful to minors."

Excerpted from Marilyn C. Mazur and Joan E. Bertin, "Sex and Censorship: Dangers to Minors and Others?" an online article from www.ncac.org/sex&censorship.html, March 1999. Reprinted with permission from the National Coalition Against Censorship.

Parents are understandably and rightly concerned about their children's sexual decisions and behavior. For some parents, sex is something reserved only for adults, limited to certain circumstances and relationships. Other adults and children have different values, goals and expectations. One rule plainly does not fit all, so how are questions about what kind of information about sex is harmful—or essential—to minors to be resolved?

Noted children's author Judy Blume has observed that "children are inexperienced, but they are not innocent." Children live in a world in which sex education is censored, but sex is glamorized in advertisements and on television, and the sexual activities of government officials are described in the morning papers and the evening news. Sexually transmitted diseases and unwanted pregnancy are other realities familiar to many teenagers. In the absence of empirical evidence demonstrating harm, perhaps it is time to reconsider whether it is constitutional—or wise—to deny young people access to information they need to make informed decisions and appropriate choices.

Sex, Sexuality, and the Law

All but the most astute legal scholars are confused. What is the legal definition of obscenity? How is it different from pornography? What is child pornography? What is the meaning of terms like "harmful to minors," and which images are considered "indecent"?

The laws regulating material with sexual content have become increasingly complex, but sex is by no means a new subject in censorship law. Americans are heir to a tradition, fostered by religious perspectives, that viewed sex as something to be tolerated, at best—a necessary evil. In the 19th century, Anthony Comstock, founder of the New York Society for the Suppression of Vice, campaigned on the slogan "Morals, Not Art and Literature" for censorship laws to suppress erotic subject matter in art and literature and information about sexuality, reproduction and birth control. The Comstock Act of 1873 banned all material found to be "lewd," "indecent," "filthy" or "obscene," including such classics as Chaucer's *Canterbury Tales*. At one time or another, books by Ernest Hemingway, D.H. Lawrence, John Steinbeck, F. Scott Fitzgerald and a host of other literary greats have been banned under obscenity laws. Legal attitudes only began to change officially in 1957, when the Supreme Court acknowledged that sex is "a great and mysterious motive force in human life."

The legal definition of obscenity has gone through several permutations, with its current definition embodied in the 1973 case, *Miller v. California*. Material with sexual content falls outside the protection of the First Amendment if 1) the work, taken as a whole, appeals to a prurient interest in sex, as judged by contemporary community standards, 2) it portrays sexual conduct, defined by law, in a patently offensive

"Sex is by no means a new subject in censorship law."

manner, and 3) the work lacks serious literary, artistic, political or scientific value. Pornography—jokingly referred to by lawyer and author Marjorie Heins as "the dreaded 'P' word"—is not the same as obscenity. Pornography is erotic material or material that arouses sexual desire. In contrast with obscenity, pornography enjoys First Amendment protection because it does not satisfy the *Miller* standard, either because it has artistic, literary, historical or other social value, or because it is not patently offensive under community standards—even if some may find it so, or because the work taken as a whole does not appeal exclusively to a prurient interest in sex. Much of the material that is targeted as "indecent" is protected, at least for adults.

Restricting Minors' Access

Children, however, are another story. Five years before *Miller*, the Court articulated a different standard for minors' access to sexual material. In *Ginsberg v. New York*, the Court upheld a New York statute criminalizing distribution of material deemed "harmful to minors" (under 17), reasoning:

> . . . the concept of obscenity or of unprotected matter may vary according to the group to whom the questionable material is directed. . . . Because of the State's exigent interest in preventing distribution to children of objectionable material, it can exercise its power to protect the health, safety, welfare and morals of its community by barring the distribution to children of books recognized to be suitable for adults.

Material may thus be deemed "harmful to minors" if it appeals to the "prurient, shameful or morbid" interest of minors, lacks serious social value for minors, and is "patently offensive" based on adult views of what is fit for minors. This "variable obscenity" standard has been faulted because it upholds "unlawful to minors" laws without requiring the government to prove a compelling state interest or actual harm. It arguably applies equally to an emancipated 16-year-old and a 4-year-old child.

Ginsberg limited minors' access to material with sexual content, but that is not the end of the story. In *New York v. Ferber*, the Court also upheld restrictions on various *depictions* of minors that are or could be considered sexual. The Court recognized the potential overbreadth of the statute—which could apply not only to child pornography, but also to a *National Geographic* photographic essay on tribal rites, ancient Greek art, and textbooks showing the effects of child sexual abuse or genital mutilation—but upheld it, citing the compelling need to protect actual children from possible exploitation by child pornographers. Left open was the question whether material apparently prohibited under the statute would be protected if it had literary, historical, scientific, or artistic value. That question remains unanswered, but since then the Court has demonstrated continued concern about possible exploitation of children used to create sexual materials, and upheld a law criminalizing an adult's *possession* of child pornography in his own home.

Court Rulings on Obscenity

These issues are in the forefront of a current debate over the Child Pornography Protection Act of 1996. The CPPA criminalizes not only sexual images involving actual children, but also computer-generated images, the use of "body doubles," and sexual images that appear to be minors, or that are advertised as minors, even if no minors are actually involved. Thus far, however, the statute has fared relatively well in the few courts to consider it. One federal district court found it unconstitutionally vague and overbroad, in a decision reversed on appeal, and another upheld the statute on the theory that such materials facilitate sexual exploitation of children. The CPPA signals a significant shift. A computer-generated image of a minor portrayed in a sexual manner is not the same as a picture of an actual child, and raises wholly different concerns from those expressed by the Court in *Ferber* and *Osborne*—the

> *"In contrast with obscenity, pornography enjoys First Amendment protection . . . because it has artistic, literary, historical or other social value."*

protection of real children from possible exploitation. The CPPA represents an unprecedented effort to suppress the ability to explore the *idea* of minors as sexual actors through pictures, film and theater. Without a recognition that the First Amendment protects such materials if they have artistic, historical, scientific, literary or other value, the CPPA could influence how *Romeo and Juliet* is presented, chill display of art like Balthus' *The Guitar Lesson*, and discourage exhibits of ancient and contemporary erotic art and statuary. It has already affected U.S. distribution of a new film version of *Lolita*, and emboldened authorities in Oklahoma to seize the film of Gunter Grass' classic World War II novel, *The Tin Drum*.

The notion of "variable obscenity," and the Court's willingness to alter the terms of First Amendment analysis in cases involving minors as observers and objects in art and literature with sexual themes also helps explain *Federal Communications Commission v. Pacifica*, where the Court upheld an FCC broadcast rule banning "indecent" speech or "patently offensive depictions or descriptions of sexual or excretory activities or organs," except on supposedly child-free "safe harbor" late night hours. The FCC's action against Pacifica Radio targeted comedian George Carlin's "Filthy Words" monologue, whose clearly satiric nature was apparently lost on the FCC and the Supreme Court, much as the anti-Nazi message of *The Tin Drum* was lost on the police in Oklahoma City.

Although the Supreme Court has generally endorsed increasingly restrictive laws wherever children and sex were combined, [in 1997] it refused to apply the *Pacifica* child-protective rationale to sex on the Internet. In *Reno v. ACLU*, the Court struck down the Communications Decency Act which targeted "indecent" speech on-line. Granting cyberspace the highest level of First Amendment protection, the Court also took the occasion to comment on the positive social value of sexually explicit speech, declaring that terms like "indecent" and "patently offensive" are so broad and vague as to threaten "serious discussion about birth control practices," homosexuality, prison rape, or safer sex in addition to "artistic images that include nude subjects" and "arguably the card catalogue of the Carnegie Library." Perhaps this represents a turning point in the Court's willingness to scrutinize more closely claims about "harm to minors," and to evaluate more seriously their independent need for access to materials with sexual content.

The uncertainty may be resolved soon. In October 1998, Congress enacted the Child Online Protection Act, also called "CDA II" because it is a successor to the Communications Decency Act. It would prohibit material deemed "harmful to minors" on commercial sites on the Internet. The President signed the bill, notwithstanding the fact that the United States Department of Justice expressed reservations about its constitutionality. Almost immediately, the law was challenged on the ground that it violates the First Amendment, as applied by the Supreme Court in *Reno v. ACLU*; the federal district court hearing the challenge has so far agreed that it is constitutionally suspect. [As of January 2000, the bill had not been enforced.] . . .

Nudity Has Become Overly Sexualized

Nudity—frontal or otherwise—involving sexual activity or otherwise has always offended a certain number of people. But shifting standards of what is acceptable for family viewing and of what is "harmful to minors" has lowered the threshold so that today it seems as if the body itself has become taboo. Nudity has been sexualized.

Frontal nudity is not tantamount to obscenity. Indeed, in much classic art, the nude form is neither erotic nor offensive. Nonetheless, distribution of pictures depicting nudity *could* be considered illegal under a variety of existing statutes and standards. Child pornography statutes have been used to target artists whose work involves children, and even parents who take pictures of their own children.

> *"The [Child Pornography Protection Act] represents an unprecedented effort to suppress the ability to explore the idea of minors as sexual actors."*

In a well-publicized case, prosecutors charged Barnes & Noble with violating state law by displaying Jock Sturges books with photographs of nude children where minors could see them. Sturges, an award-winning photographer whose work is in the Museum of Modern Art, the Metropolitan Museum of Art and the Bibliotheque National of Paris, has been targeted by Focus on the Family and Loyal Opposition, headed by Randall Terry, former leader of the anti-abortion group Operation Rescue. . . . Some of the charges against Barnes & Noble have been dropped, after it agreed to display Sturges books higher than five and a half feet, while others are still pending. Other less visible cases have turned an innocent picture-taking session into a nightmare, like that experienced by a Wayne State University art professor, who was investigated for child abuse when a janitor found a nude photograph of her three-year-old child in her wastebasket.

Books and photographs are not the only focus of such attacks. The Academy-Award winning film, *The Tin Drum*, was seized from the Oklahoma City library, private homes and video stores because of complaints by Oklahomans for Children and Families. The film's message, about the disintegration of central Europe during the rise of Naziism, was completely overlooked by OCAF in its attack on a few isolated and suggestive, but not explicit, scenes. A federal judge ruled that the police violated the Constitution when they seized copies of the film without a warrant or court order, and more recently held that the film does not violate the state's law against child pornography.

> **"Sometimes efforts to protect minors from nudity and sexual knowledge verge on the ludicrous."**

Another artistic casualty of the sex and censorship wars is the new film version of *Lolita*, starring Jeremy Irons. True to the Nabokov novel, the film explores a man's sexual obsession with a prepubescent but precocious girl, and uses a body double in sexually explicit scenes. Although the film has been shown in Europe, *Lolita* has until recently been unable to find a distributor in the U.S., undoubtedly because of uncertainty about whether it will elicit charges of child pornography.

What of *National Geographic* pictures of naked children involved in tribal rituals? Medical textbooks displaying children's genitals? Scholarly description of children's sexual fantasies? Could these be construed to violate state pornography statutes which prohibit "lascivious exhibition of genitalia"? That questions like these exist is enough to predict a chilling effect on scholarly writing and distribution of such materials. The ambiguity of the legal standards, the absence of any limiting principle that protects work with artistic, scholarly or other merit, and vagueness about what is harmful to minors all plainly contribute to censorship.

Problematic and Absurd Censorship

Most problematic is the idea that children shouldn't see a depiction of a naked body. Consider the decision by one TV station to cancel an educational film teaching women breast self-examination techniques because the broadcaster decided the material was "inappropriate for family viewing." This was the same theory on which the New York State Museum recently asked sculptor Kim Waale to remove portions of her work, *A Good Look: The Adolescent Bedroom Project*. Similarly, many libraries have "no nudes" policies for their pub-

lic exhibit space, resulting in the exclusion of Robin Bellospirito's highly styl-
ized nudes. Tulane student artist Jenny Root's nude sculpture, *Mother/Father*,
was moved so it wouldn't accidentally be seen by children. The aversion to
artistic representations of the human body reached new heights at Brigham
Young University, where four sculptures of nudes, including *The Kiss*, were removed from a traveling Rodin exhibit. Bellospirito won her right to exhibit her
paintings in court; Waale and two other artists withdrew their work from the
New York State Museum in protest, but art lovers in Utah who hoped to see *The
Kiss* were out of luck.

Sometimes efforts to protect minors from nudity and sexual knowledge
verge on the ludicrous. On Long Island, an edition of *Where's Waldo?*, the
charming mini figure puzzle book, was banned because hidden among hundreds of tiny figures crammed onto the "beach" page someone found a woman
with a partially exposed breast the size of a pencil tip. In Erie, Pennsylvania,
teachers used markers to block out passages of mating habits from naturalist
Diane Fossey's *Gorillas in the Mist*. In New York, a teacher was disciplined
for allowing other students to read a composition about a sexual experience
written by a fellow student. In Octorara, Pennsylvania, school officials removed a Margaret Atwood story, "Rape Fantasies," from the high school hon-
ors English curriculum.

Nudity is opposed on both sides of
the ideological spectrum. Goya's famous *Nude Maja*, hung on a classroom wall for 15 years until a pro-

> **"Morality is not the
> province of the far right."**

fessor charged that it was "sexually harassing." In New York City new zoning
rules will exile to remote areas most sex shops, topless clubs, and bookstores
featuring sexually explicit but constitutionally protected fare. The language of
the ordinance is broad enough to apply not only to "peep shows," but also to a
smash hit like *Oh! Calcutta!* or an art gallery specializing in nude art; it was
recently declared constitutional by a federal appeals court.

While the religious right is fueling much of the effort to ban these materials
from our communities, the religious community is by no means monolithic in
its views. Consider the exuberant Sister Wendy who charmed millions with her
TV programs on the history of art, including many nude and sexually explicit
works. Consider, too, the highly touted sex education programs embraced by
religious people and organizations, including American Baptists and the Unitar-
ian Universalists. Morality is not the province of the far right, and repression of
information about sex and sexuality and of images of nudity in art is not universally accepted as correct by all religions. . . .

By relaxing the standards for judging censorship where minors and sex are
involved, the courts have invited some of the disarray now apparent in sex education, community access to art, and minors' access to information about sex,

health and the body. Until courts begin to scrutinize the question of what is "harmful to minors" more closely, students may miss out on an important part of the education they need to prepare for life; artists and art lovers will continue to experience the chill of uncertainty, and the entire community will remain vulnerable to those who charge that protection of minors requires a fig leaf on Michelangelo's *David*, [and] a bikini on Matisse's *Blue Nude*.

Internet Filters Should Not Be Used

by Barbara Miner

About the author: *Barbara Miner is the managing editor of* Rethinking Schools.

Imagine if an unknown person came into your school library every month and removed books from the shelves. You would never be told which books were being taken or why, other than that someone, somewhere, deemed them "inappropriate," "indecent," "radical," "tasteless," or "gross." Imagine if the books included works on the Holocaust, Islam, AIDS/HIV, gay rights, the National Organization for Women, or the International Workers of the World union.

Couldn't ever happen? Guess again.

Filters Block More than Pornography

Under the guise of protecting children from "smut" and "indecency," Internet filtering programs routinely block access to thousands of World Wide Web pages, chat rooms, newsgroups and other Internet options—including the topics listed above. What's more, if Sen. John McCain (R-Ariz.) gets his way, Congress will pass legislation mandating that school districts must use filtering software if they want to receive discounts on telecommunications services, or what is known as the E-rate. [As of January 2000, that legislation had not been passed.]

Groups fighting censorship, in particular organizations which want to nurture the democratic potential of the Internet, are hoping to scuttle the legislation. They also want to alert the public to the dark underside of seemingly innocuous filtering programs.

"The word 'filter' is much too kind to these programs. It conjures up inaccurate, gee-whiz images of sophisticated, discerning choice," Seth Finkelstein, a founder of The Censorware Project, said in testimony on the McCain bill [in spring 1998]. "When these products are examined in detail, they usually turn out to be the crudest of blacklists, long tables of hapless material which has run

Reprinted from Barbara Miner, "Internet Filtering: Beware the Cybercensors," *Rethinking Schools*, Summer 1998. Reprinted with permission from *Rethinking Schools*.

afoul of a stupid computer program or person, perhaps offended by the word 'breast' (as in possibly 'breast cancer') . . . ."

Such warnings are more than political rhetoric. Every filtering program that has been examined in detail, for instance, has placed feminist organizations on its list of censored sites, according to The Censorware Project, an on-line group founded by computer software experts, free speech advocates, and Internet activists. A number of filtering software companies have even blocked sites reporting on political and technical problems with the software.

Filtering programs are "a bait-and-switch maneuver," argue Brock Meeks and Declan McCullagh, authors of a 1996 filtering exposé in the e-mail publication *CyberWire Dispatch.* "The smut-censors say they're going after porn, but they quietly restrict political speech."

Michael Sims of The Censorware Project cautions that people need to be skeptical of claims by filtering companies that they are technically capable of thoughtfully reviewing the millions of pages on the World Wide Web. "Everyone knows that a standard automobile doesn't get 200 miles per gallon of gas, so that claim is unrealistic," Sims told *Rethinking Schools.* "But people don't understand that some of the claims of censorware makers are equally unrealistic."

The Communications Decency Act

Protecting children from pornography on the Internet is clearly an important issue. The discussion, however, has been dominated by fear, scare stories, and political posturing. Opponents of censorship are especially worried that some groups, especially politicians and organizations affiliated with the religious right, are using legitimate concerns about protecting children to push through a broader agenda of "cleaning up" the free-wheeling world of the Internet and imposing a moralistically and politically narrow view of the world.

One of the most important Internet censorship battles involved the Communications Decency Act (CDA). Passed by Congress in the fall of 1996, the bill would, in practice, have banned "indecency" from the Internet as a way of protecting children from "patently offensive" material. Those sections of the law involving the Internet were found unconstitutional by the U.S. Supreme Court in June of 1997. The CDA was "a creature of the religious right, which had a significant hand in sculpting it, lining up politicians to support it, and then supplying them with the ammunition they needed to get it passed," according to Jonathan Wallace, author of the book *Sex, Laws, and Cyberspace* and a founder of the Internet magazine *The Ethical Spectacle.*

> *"Every filtering program that has been examined in detail, . . . has placed feminist organizations on its list of censored sites."*

The U.S. Supreme Court's decision on the CDA has been called "the first free speech ruling of the 21st Century." In it, the court argues that the Internet is akin to printed material, not to radio or television, and deserves the highest free speech protections. It reiterates that the Internet "is a unique and wholly new medium of worldwide human communication," and that it is "no exaggeration to conclude that the content on the Internet is as diverse as human thought." (The beginning pages of the majority decision are a wonderful summary of the Internet's origins, scope and potential. The ruling can be downloaded from: http://supct.law.cornell.edu/supct/html/96-511.ZO.html.)

> *"Protecting children from pornography on the Internet is clearly an important issue. The discussion, however, has been dominated by fear, scare stories, and political posturing."*

Both sides in the CDA suit stipulated as fact that, while pornography is available on the web, almost all sexually explicit images are preceded by warnings. The "odds are slim" that users would encounter such material accidentally, according to the court.

Reactions for and Against Filtering

Having been set back in the courts, religious right groups and their allies turned toward imposing filtering software in public libraries and schools. In a typical story, the conservative *Washington Times* wrote a story in October 1997 with the headline: "Cyberporn at libraries has smut foes furious: We need to keep pornography out of taxpayer facilities." A story that December in the *Weekly Standard* was titled: "Quiet in the Library! Children Viewing Porn." The magazine, generally considered the leading conservative newsweekly, criticized the American Library Association for its concern with censorship and the use of filtering software in public libraries. It then asked:

> So, what should conservatives do in response? They could adopt a libertarian stance: shut down the libraries and let citizens do their own Web searches at home, with or without filters. Or they could try to take the libraries back from the American Library Association; perhaps local politicians could fire recalcitrant librarians, which would free up cash for computer-equipped charter schools whose librarians treat parents' concerns with respect. The Republican Congress could pass a law that helps parents sue librarians who fail to take reasonable measures [against indecency] . . . Congress could even go a step further and prod the Justice Department to jail careless librarians when the computers under their charge are used to break the law.

It's not surprising that many school districts have decided to use filtering software. Given legitimate concerns about protecting children from pornography and age-inappropriate material, coupled with the highly charged political atmosphere that surrounds all school issues, they may feel that they have little choice. "Obviously, schools need to be concerned about some of the materials that people are producing that may not be appropriate for kids," notes Gary Marx of the American Association of School Administrators. "If schools don't worry about it, then they will be told very quickly by people in the community, if there is an incident, that they had better be concerned."

As more information becomes available about filtering software, a growing number of media, education, and computer groups are advising caution. For instance, the Journalism Education Association, which represents middle and high school journalism teachers and advisors for school papers, passed a resolution in November that "strongly opposes the use of filters or blocking software." Other groups concerned about filtering software range from the American Society of Newspaper Editors to Computer Professionals for Social Responsibility, Feminists for Free Expression, the PEN American Center, and the Society of Professional Journalists.

The controversy centers around the use of filtering software by governmental bodies such as public libraries or school districts. The fear is that in using the software, the libraries and schools put themselves in the position of allowing the filter to act as a censor.

Critics of filtering software make two main points. First, school districts and public libraries need to be aware of how filtering works—that it blocks out any number of legitimate sites and, conversely, often fails to block "indecent" sites. Second, particularly for schools, using filters may be at the expense of the more educationally sound practice of teaching kids how to responsibly use and evaluate the Internet. (This viewpoint focuses on filtering software; an equally important issue for school districts is developing "Appropriate Use Policies" that govern a range of Internet issues, from student use of e-mail, to recreational versus educational use of the Internet at school, to disciplinary actions when Internet policies are violated. One of the most important issues is teaching children safety issues on the Internet—for example, that they should never give out their name, phone number, or address to strangers on the net.)

> *"Schools and libraries have to take on faith that the filtering company is doing a good job. That faith may be misplaced, however."*

How Filtering Software Works

Some of the major filtering software products are CYBERsitter, Cyber Patrol, Net Nanny, BESS, X-Stop, SmartFilter and SafeSurf. The software is produced by private companies which, in order to protect and sell their product, don't want to be too specific about how the software works or release a list of what sites are blocked.

But just suppose a librarian or school official did get a copy of the blacklist. They probably wouldn't have time to evaluate it thoroughly. Cyber Patrol claims to have over 50,000 blocked entries, and each entry can ban as little as one web page or as much as an entire domain. At a minute per entry, that's more than 100 workdays just to give a cursory inspection, according to Finkelstein of The Censorware Project. A few minutes of math calculations "should immediately destroy the myth that a librarian or schoolteacher can look over a product and make more than insignificant adjustments for his or her own values," Finkelstein argues.

> *"If the goal is protecting children from pornography, many of the filtering softwares don't block what should be blocked."*

As a result, schools and libraries have to take on faith that the filtering company is doing a good job. That faith may be misplaced, however.

A growing number of organizations are investigating and exposing how filtering software works. One such group is the cyber-organization Peacefire: Youth Alliance Against Internet Censorship. The group was founded in August 1996 to represent students' and minors' interests in the debate over freedom of speech on the Internet. Full membership is limited to people under 21. On its web site, Peacefire notes: "There were very few people in mid-1996 speaking out against blocking software programs like CYBERsitter and Cyber Patrol, because most adults would not be affected by the proliferation of these programs." (Anyone interested in not only filtering software but the power of youth organizing should check out Peacefire's site: www.peacefire.org.)

Peacefire maintains a list of some of the sites blocked by various filters. One of the more far-reaching filtering programs appears to be CYBERsitter, which has been marketed in part by the religious right organization Focus on the Family. In its options for filtering, CYBERsitter includes the categories, "advocating illegal/radical activities" and "gay/lesbian activities."

Blocked Sites

Some of the sites that have been blocked by CYBERsitter include:
• The National Organization for Women
• The International Gay and Lesbian Human Rights Commission
• Yahoo web search for "gay rights"
• The Peacefire web site

CYBERsitter apparently was upset with Peacefire because of its exposé of blocked sites. CYBERsitter even went to Peacefire's Internet provider, Media3, and threatened to block the pages of all the other domain names on the Media3 server if Peacefire were not removed from the server, according to an article in the Dec. 6, 1996, *WIRED News*. Media3 threatened legal action if CYBERsitter followed through on its threats.

One of the first articles to blow the whistle on filtering programs was the *CyberWire Dispatch* article "Keys to the Kingdom" (available at www.eff.org/pub/Publications/Declan_McCullagh/cwd.keys.to.the.kingdom.0796.article). "CYBERsitter doesn't hide the fact that they're trying to enforce a moral code," according to the article. When CYBERsitter CEO Brian Milburn was asked about the National Organization for Women's (NOW) concern that its site was blocked, he responded, "If NOW doesn't like it, tough. . . . We have not and will not bow to any pressure from any organization that disagrees with our philosophy."

Other software filtering companies may be less overtly political but they nonetheless have blocked a range of worthwhile pages. Take Cyber Patrol. According to Peacefire, sites and newsgroups that have been blocked by Cyber Patrol include:

- The MIT Student Association for Freedom of Expression
- Planned Parenthood
- Nizkor, a Holocaust remembrance page
- Envirolink, a clearinghouse of environmental information on the Internet
- *Mother Jones* magazine online
- The soc.feminism newsgroup
- The AOL Sucks web site ("Why American Online Sucks")

(If you want to check out these filtering programs, go to their websites. For CYBERsitter it's www.solidoak.com; for Cyber Patrol it's www.cyberpatrol.com. The Cyber Patrol logo is telling: It consists of a police-type badge and the slogan: "To Surf and Protect.")

Questionable Standards

CyberWire Dispatch calls Cyber Patrol "easily the largest and most extensive smut-blocker. It assigns each undesirable website to at least one and often multiple categories that range from 'violence/profanity' to 'sexual acts,' 'drugs and drug culture,' and 'gross depictions.'" What, one might ask, constitutes "gross depictions"? One answer is, animal rights pages—such as a blocked page which shows syphilis-infected monkeys.

Wallace, of *The Ethical Spectacle,* points out the tendency of filters to block based on political content. His magazine—which he describes as "a sober, intellectual, rather dry publication, without prurient photographs or stories, which aspires to be an electronic equivalent of print magazines like *The Nation, The National Review,* or *The Atlantic*—has been blocked by seven censorware products. "And those are only the ones I know about," he says.

Finkelstein of The Censorware Project notes that Cyber Patrol blocked his site on Internet Labeling and Rating Systems (part of the MIT Student Association for Freedom of Expression, www.mit.edu/activities/safe), under categories ranging from Full Nudity to Militant/Extreme to Satanic/Cult.

Blocking worthwhile pages is only part of the problem. If the goal is protecting children from pornography, many of the filtering softwares don't block what should be blocked. An article in the *Focus on the Family* magazine noted that *Consumer Reports* tested four of the biggest Internet filters. "The results were discouraging," according to *Focus on the Family.* "After selecting 22 'easy-to-find' objectionable Web sites, technical experts attempted to log onto those sites with the blocking software running. SurfWatch tested the best, with only four sites getting past the software. Cyber Patrol let six sites slip through, CYBERsitter missed eight, and Net Nanny let all 22 through."

The *Focus on the Family* article also complained that filtering software had blocked "Christian videos that deal with sexuality."

Why Filters Are Too Broad

One of the unanswered questions about filtering software is: who decides and how? Filtering software companies make it seem that decisions are being carefully made by reasonable people whose only goal is protecting children. But in reality, filtering software generally relies on scanning a site's keywords or its URL, rather than actually looking at a site. That is why, for example, if a filtering software is looking to block anything with the word "sex," it will potentially eliminate sites about Middlesex, England or the poetry of Anne Sexton.

The article "Keys to the Kingdom" notes that Cyber Patrol doesn't even store the complete URL for blocking and instead abbreviates the last three characters. Thus, for instance, Shawn Knight had an occult resources page, located at Carnegie Mellon University, and the final coding for his site began with the letters "sha." Cyber Patrol blocked 23 other accounts at Carnegie Mellon University with "sha" as the first three letters of the final coding—including Derrick "Shadow" Brasherr's web page on Pittsburgh radio stations. When the filter blocked the "CyberOS" gay video available through the Internet Service Provider webcom.com, it also blocked 17 other sites at the server that started with "cyb"—including a site billed as the first "Cyber High School."

The sheer immensity of the web—a recent study in the journal *Science* estimates there are roughly 320 million separate web pages—makes human evaluation of web pages impossible, according to Internet experts. Sims of The Censorware Project notes that Digital Equipment Corporation's search engine AltaVista—perhaps the fastest search engine, with a bandwidth so powerful it could support 87 million phone lines—adds a new page in a fraction of a second and still only has

> *"Filtering can be compared to taking books out of the library and storing them in an inaccessible back room."*

about 28% of the web in its database. "No censorware company has more than a tiny fraction of AltaVista's bandwidth," Sims notes. "No censorware company has more than a fraction of the hardware, or technical expertise, of the people at Digital Equipment Corporation. And supposedly these pages are viewed by a human, taking a minute or more instead of a split second?"

It is "mathematically impossible to 'view' any significant portion of the web," according to Sims.

Family Friendly Search Engines

Ever on the prowl for a new product or gimmick to sell to parents and schools, computer software companies are developing "family friendly search engines." If filtering can be compared to taking books out of the library and storing them in an inaccessible back room, "family friendly search engines" are akin to taking students to the Library of Congress but not letting them use the card catalog.

What is being billed as "the world's first family friendly Internet search site" was released this past October by Net Shepherd and AltaVista and called Net Shepherd Family Search. According to Net Shepherd's web site, the search engine filters out web sites "judged by an independent panel of demographically appropriate Internet users, to be inappropriate and/or objectionable to the average user families."

The Electronic Privacy Information Center (EPIC), a Washington, D.C.–based public interest research center established in 1994, has released a study on Net Shepherd's Family Search engine. In the study, it conducted 100 searches using AltaVista, a traditional search engine, and Net Shepherd's Family Search. Requests ranged from phrases such as "American Red Cross," to the "San Diego Zoo," to the "Smithsonian Institution," to potentially controversial topics such as the "Bill of Rights," "Christianity" and "eating disorders."

"In every case in our sample, we found that the family friendly search engine prevented us from obtaining access to almost 90% of the materials on the Internet containing the relevant search terms," according to EPIC. "We further found that in many cases, the search service denied access to 99% of the material that would otherwise be available without the filters." For example:

• The non-filtered search for "NAACP" listed 4,000 documents. The Family Search produced 15 documents.

• The non-filtered search for "Thomas Edison" came up with 11,552 documents. On Family Search: nine.

And poor Dr. Seuss. Only eight of the 2,653 references on AltaVista relating to Dr. Seuss were available through Family Search—and one of them was a parody of a Dr. Seuss story using details from the murder of Nicole Brown Simpson.

"While it is true that there is material available on the Internet that some will find legitimately objectionable, it is also clear that in some cases the proposed solutions may be worse than the actual problem," EPIC noted. The most important task is for parents and teachers to take an active role in guiding children's use of the Internet. As EPIC notes: "Helping children tell right from wrong is not something that should be left to computer software or search engines."

Chapter 4

Should the Government Regulate Art and Popular Culture?

Chapter Preface

Artists have long sought the aid of patrons to fund their work. For example, the famous composer Ludwig van Beethoven had several benefactors, including Vienna's Prince Carl Lichnowsky. In modern America, artists and museums frequently receive funding from the government. This patronage can come with strings attached, however, because art that is considered offensive may risk losing its funding. Such an incident occurred in fall 1999, when New York City mayor Rudolph W. Giuliani cut the city's funding of the Brooklyn Museum of Art by one-third of the museum's $24 million annual budget. Giuliani's action was prompted by his disapproval of the exhibit "Sensation"—particularly a painting by Chris Ofili called "Holy Virgin Mary," which consists of a black Virgin Mary decorated with pieces of elephant dung and sexually-explicit pictures. The museum sued the mayor, and a federal judge found in its favor on November 1, 1999, declaring that the mayor had violated the First Amendment and ordering him to restore full funding to the museum. The judge may have had the last word, but he and Giuliani were not the only people who debated whether the exhibit should receive public funds.

Many commentators contended that Ofili's painting was offensive, particularly to Catholics, and that public funds should not be used to support such an exhibit. They argue that private museums and commercial galleries are more appropriate places to display Ofili's work. Joseph Perkins, a columnist for the *San Diego Union-Tribune*, writes: "One needn't be Catholic to find Ofili's painting offensive. The art elite may consider it some kind of contemporary masterpiece. But when you really get down to it, it's simply a hate crime masquerading as art." Perkins contends that asking Catholics and offended non-Catholics to fund the exhibit is as absurd as asking Jews to fund the painting of swastikas on synagogues.

However, other writers assert that "Holy Virgin Mary" is not an affront to Catholicism and that "Sensation" should not be censored. Katha Pollitt, a writer for the *Nation*, contends: "It's absurd to call it anti-Catholic—Chris Ofili . . . is himself a practicing Catholic." Pollitt also notes that Ofili has used elephant dung in paintings of African American musicians Miles Davis and James Brown, but those works have not been criticized. Charles Levendosky of the *Star-Tribune* in Casper, Wyoming, maintains that "city officials cannot renege on the subsidies simply because they don't like the art exhibited in the museums. Government censorship violates the First Amendment."

Although the controversy over the exhibition has died down, the debate over whether art and popular culture should be regulated continues. In the following chapter, the authors consider whether government, parents, or businesses should regulate art.

Artists Overstate the Effects of Government Regulation

by Roger Kimball

About the author: *Roger Kimball is managing editor of* The New Criterion.

Anyone with a taste for absurdity will find much to admire in the more 'advanced' precincts of the contemporary art world. There are, first of all, the many grotesque elements of the spectacle: government-funded 'performance' artists (or do I mean performance 'artists'?) who smear themselves with chocolate and then prance about haranguing their audiences about the evils of patriarchy, capitalism, etc (Karen Finley); conceptual artists who conceal themselves under a false floor in an art gallery, masturbating continuously for hours on end while broadcasting their sighs and whispers to gallery-goers who tread unknowingly above them (Vito Acconci); pathetic figures, like the chap whose most famous piece featured himself nailed to an automobile (Chris Burden); and then there are the miscellaneous knaves and charlatans of all description, the battalions of eager hucksters who make up for their lack of talent and artistic accomplishment with a combination of egotism, shamelessness, and an acute sense of marketing.

The cornucopia of absurdity that the art world has become offers hours of entertainment to the student of human fatuousness. Not, of course, that all artists contribute to this degraded and degrading sideshow. But here we must distinguish quite sharply between the serious life of art, which pursues its own course, and the chic purlieus of the 'cutting-edge,' which are corrupted by a rebarbative academic hermeticism on the one side and an addiction to extremity on the other. It is of course cutting-edge art that gets all the attention, that infests the galleries of SoHo and TriBeCa (and Cork Street), that garners grants from the National Endowment of the Arts, and gets written up in reader-proof journals like *Artforum* and *October*. If there were a nationwide moratorium on

Reprinted from Roger Kimball, "Uncensored and Unashamed," *Index on Censorship*, May/June 1996. Reprinted with permission from *Index on Censorship*. For more information call 011 44 (207) 278-2313, fax 011 44 (207) 278-1878, e-mail: contact@indexoncensorship.org, or visit www.indexoncensorship.org.

the use of words like 'transgressive,' denizens of the art world would be instantly out of business. For what they traffic in is not art but a species of cultural politics that poaches on the authority of art in order, first, to enhance its prestige (and its prices) and, second, to purchase immunity from certain forms of criticism.

The Unfortunate Results of Avant-Garde Art

To a large extent, the calamities of art today are due to the aftermath of the avant-garde: to all those 'adversarial' gestures, poses, ambitions, and tactics that emerged and were legitimised in the 1880s and 1890s, flowered in the first half of this century, and that live a sort of posthumous existence now in the frantic twilight of postmodernism. In part, our present situation, like avant-garde itself, is a complication (not to say a perversion) of our Romantic inheritance. The elevation of art from a didactic pastime to a prime spiritual resource, the self-conscious probing of inherited forms and artistic strictures, the image of the artist as a tortured, oppositional figure: all achieve a first maturity in Romanticism. These themes were exacerbated as the avant-garde developed from an impulse to a movement and finally into a tradition of its own.

The French critic Albert Thibaudet summarised some of the chief features of this burgeoning tradition in his reflections on the Symbolist movement in literature. Writing in 1936, Thibaudet noted that Symbolism 'accustomed literature to the idea of indefinite revolution' and inaugurated a 'new climate' in French literature: a climate characterised by 'the chronic avant-gardism of poetry, the "What's new?" of the "informed" public, . . . the proliferation of schools and manifestos,' and the ambition 'to occupy that extreme point, to attain for an hour that crest of the wave in a tossing sea. The Symbolist revolution,' Thibaudet concluded, 'might perhaps have been definitively the last, because it incorporated the theme of chronic revolution into the normal condition of literature.' The problem is that the avant-garde has become a casualty of its own success. Having won battle after battle, it gradually transformed a recalcitrant bourgeois culture into a willing collaborator in its raids on established taste. But in this victory were the seeds of its own irrelevance, for without credible resistance, its oppositional gestures degenerated into a kind of aesthetic buffoonery. In this sense, the institutionalisation of the avant-garde—what the critic Clement Greenberg called 'avant-gardism'—spells the death, or at least the senility, of the avant-garde.

> *"The cornucopia of absurdity that the art world has become offers hours of entertainment to the student of human fatuousness."*

As the search for something new to say or do becomes ever more desperate, artists push themselves to make extreme gestures simply in order to be noticed. But an inexorably self-defeating logic has taken hold here: at a time when so much art is routinely extreme and audiences have become inured to the most brutal spectacles, extremity itself becomes a commonplace. After one has had oneself nailed to a Volkswagen, what's left? Having oneself nailed to a Rolls Royce? A Chevy? A Volvo? A Citroën? Without the sustaining, authoritative backdrop of the normal, extreme gestures—stylistic, moral, political—degenerate into a grim species of mannerism. Lacking any guiding aesthetic imperative, such gestures, no matter how shocking or repulsive they may be, are so many exercises in futility.

It is in part to compensate for this encroaching futility that the desire to marry art and politics has become such a prominent feature of the contemporary art scene. When the artistic significance of art is at a minimum, politics rushes in to fill the void. From the crude political allegories of a Leon Golub or Hans Haacke to the feminist sloganeering of Jenny Holzer, Karen Finley, or Cindy Sherman, much that goes under the name of art today is incomprehensible without reference to its political content. Indeed, in many cases what we see are nothing but political gestures that poach on the prestige of art in order to enhance their authority. Another word for this activity is propaganda, although at a moment when so much of art is given over to propagandising the word seems inadequate. It goes without saying that the politics in question are as predictable as clockwork. Not only are they standard items on the prevailing tablet of left-wing

> *"The idea that art—or any other form of expression, for that matter—is censored in the US today is preposterous."*

pieties, they are also cartoon versions of the same. It's the political version of painting by numbers: AIDS, the homeless, 'gender politics,' the Third World and the environment line up on one side with white hats, while capitalism, patriarchy, the United States, and traditional morality and religion assemble yonder in black hats.

Art Is Not Threatened

It is in this context that we must understand the outcry over 'censorship' and freedom of expression in the American art world. I employ scare quotes because the idea that art—or any other form of expression, for that matter—is censored in the US today is preposterous. Take a trip to the local newsstand; turn on the television to MTV or any of a number of 'adult' channels; visit the Biennial exhibition of the Whitney Museum of American Art: anywhere and everywhere in American society the foulest possible language, the most graphic images of sexual congress and sexual perversion, the most inflammatory speech ridiculing political and religious leaders abounds. The heavy hand of government is happy to regulate smoking and the composition of potato crisps; it interferes not a whit with what artists and *soi-disants* artists may say or represent in their art.

And yet we again and again hear that the freedom of artists is threatened. How can this be? The controversy crystallised a few years ago over two photographers, Andres Serrano and Robert Mapplethorpe. Serrano achieved instant celebrity for *Piss Christ,* a photograph of a crucifix submerged in Mr Serrano's urine. Mapplethorpe, as all the world knows, captured the limelight with his photographs of the sado-masochistic homosexual underworld. What initially sparked controversy was not the existence or circulation of these images, but the fact that their exhibition had been partly underwritten by the National Endowment for the Arts, a governmental agency. After all, such blasphemous and perverted

> *"We were asked to believe that denying someone a government grant was tantamount to censorship and constituted a dangerous assault on the First Amendment."*

images had been circulating in the American art world for years with nary a raised eyebrow. But the revelation that these and other similar productions were being supported in part by taxpayers' dollars created a sensation.

It really was extraordinary. Overnight, it seemed, we were asked to believe that denying someone a government grant was tantamount to censorship and constituted a dangerous assault on the First Amendment. The mandarins of the art world really had a field day. In 1991, for example, *Art Journal,* an official organ of the College Art Association, the largest and most important academic organisation of art teachers in the country, devoted two issues to the issue of censorship. One of the guest editors was Robert Storr, an epitome of art-world trendiness who had recently been appointed curator at the Museum of Modern Art in New York. Mr Storr's own contribution to the issue was an essay entitled 'Art, Censorship, and the First Amendment: This Is Not a Test.' You know the script: the USA is now in the grip of a fearsome right-wing effort to suppress free speech; artists are being muzzled everywhere. 'On every front,' he wrote, 'legal challenges are being made to the freedom of serious artists, clever opportunists, dedicated amateurs, and ordinary people to represent the world as they see it.' I wish that Mr Storr could have cited one ordinary citizen, let alone one 'serious artist,' facing such 'challenges.' But of course he adduced none because none exist.

Superficial Arguments

Instead, what Mr Storr offered readers of *Art Journal* was a species of grade-school absolutism in which anything less than total freedom is rejected as intolerable repression. Accordingly, his chief concern with the First Amendment turned on the licence to utter dirty words in public. 'In the final analysis, freedom of speech isn't so much a matter of when one may legally shout "Fire!" in a crowded theatre but whether or not one may . . . yell "Shit!" on stage in a publicly funded production—or "Fuck!"'

The stunning superficiality of Mr Storr's performance was summed up in his claim that 'defending free speech depends on a willingness . . . to break taboos when and wherever they present themselves.' It is worth pausing over this statement to contemplate what the nightmare of a society without taboos might be like. For Mr Storr, however, respecting taboos is tantamount to 'repressive decorum' and 'general self-censorship.' (Is 'self-censorship' the same thing as censorship?) In order to illustrate what he has in mind by free speech, he returns to the case of Robert Mapplethorpe, the archetypal 'transgressive artist.' Why didn't the *New York Times,* which had recently run an article about the Mapplethorpe controversy by the art critic Hilton Kramer, reproduce the offending photographs? For Mr Storr, this was an instance of 'pre-emptive and accusatory squeamishness.' To make up for the omission, he did his readers the 'courtesy' of reproducing in glossy exactness Mapplethorpe's notorious *X Portfolio,* which features grisly images of sexual torture and degradation.

If the measure of art really were its capacity to offend—as Mr Storr and so many like-minded champions of the moment have been eager to assure us—then Robert Mapplethorpe's photographs would indeed be masterpieces. But offensiveness is merely offensiveness, not an index of artistic quality. And this brings us to the two key questions with which this spurious battle over censorship confronts us.

Art and Morality

The first issue concerns what we might call the moral status of art. It is widely assumed that by baptising something as 'art' we thereby exempt it from other kinds of criticism—as if an object's status as art rendered it invulnerable to extra-aesthetic censure. Some such assumption, for example, stands behind Oscar Wilde's famous observation that 'There is no such thing as a moral or an immoral book. Books are well written or badly written. That is all.' Like everything Wilde wrote, that is very nicely phrased; but the question remains, is it true? Is it true that Robert Mapplethorpe's depiction of one man urinating into another man's mouth should be judged purely in *aesthetic* terms? Dostoyevsky once wrote that 'Beauty is the battlefield where God and the Devil war for the soul of man.' It is perhaps an open question whether Robert Mapplethorpe's photographs can lay claim to beauty; but clearly they issue a moral challenge. This is why the art critic who defended Mapplethorpe's photo-

> *"In the art world today, the First Amendment is routinely invoked to justify or protect objects and behaviour whose entire raison d'être is to shock."*

graphs on 'formal' grounds, adducing in one instance the 'classical' disposition of the diagonals in a depiction of a man inserting his forearm into another man's rectum, was offering not criticism but a cynical exercise in nihilistic persiflage.

Which brings us to the second key question: the relationship between freedom of expression and the limits of acceptable behaviour. The two are not necessarily the same. As the philosopher John Searle has pointed out, 'From the proposition that one has a right to do something it does not follow that it is a right or even a morally permissible thing to do.' The fact that one has a legal right to engage in some behaviour does not necessarily make that behaviour acceptable. Searle continues: 'Any healthy human institution—family, state, university, ski team—grants its members rights that far exceed the bounds of morally acceptable behaviour. There are many reasons for this. One is that the flexibility necessary for free, successful, and creative behaviour requires a big gulf between what the institution grants by way of rights and what it has to expect it is to succeed. The gulf between the rights granted and the performance expected is bridged by the responsibility of the members.' In the art world today, the First Amendment is routinely invoked to justify or protect objects and behaviour whose entire raison d'être is to shock and discommode. These raids on the fringes of extremity have helped to transform the art world into a moral cesspool. In testing the limits of free expression, the art world has demonstrated its emancipation from all manner of social and aesthetic norms. In the process, it has trivialised not only art but also the freedom in whose name it was created.

Government Measures Are Needed to Regulate Television

by Joan Dykstra

About the author: *Joan Dykstra is the former president of the National Parent-Teacher Association (PTA).*

Editor's Note: This viewpoint was originally testimony given before the U.S. Senate Committee on Commerce, Science and Transportation.

Mr. Chairman and members of the Senate Committee on Commerce, Science and Transportation. I am Joan Dykstra, president of the National Parent-Teacher Association (PTA). The National PTA is comprised of almost 6.8 million parents, teachers, and other child advocates concerned about improving the quality of television programming for children, youth, and their families. Thank you for this opportunity to present the views of many parents nationwide who have been frequently frustrated in their attempts to influence children's television programming while respecting First Amendment free speech protections. In addition, I would also like to thank Senators Kent Conrad and Joe Lieberman and Representatives Ed Markey and Jim Moran for their leadership in supporting a v-chip concept which employs technology allowing parents to make decisions about the programs their children watch.

This Committee has requested that I address the following concerns pertaining to the television ratings system proposed by the Television Ratings Implementation Group:

1. To what extent were the views of parents and other interested parties solicited in the creation of the ratings system and how does the proposed ratings system reflect those views;
2. Do the ratings provide enough information to enable adults to make informed judgments about the suitability of programs for children's viewing; and
3. Why weren't other rating systems selected.

Excerpted from testimony given by Joan Dykstra before the U.S. Senate Committee on Commerce, Science, and Transportation, February 27, 1997.

Important Decisions

But in order to answer these questions, permit me to remind this Committee and the television industry what is at stake. We are at a crucial and tenuous juncture pertaining to children's television. If done correctly, the system of v-chip technology will provide a balance between the industry's concern about government regulatory excesses and the public's concern about better quality programming for children and families. The v-chip can balance the industry's freedom to broadcast with the parent's right to choose; the producer's freedom to produce with the parent's right to have information about what is produced; the parent's responsibility to monitor television programming for their children with the industry's responsibility to provide a system that gives parents adequate information about the content of a program.

The decisions that will be made by the FCC and the television industry during the next several months will determine whether parents and the industry can co-exist and strike a balance without further government activity, or whether parents and the Congress will resort to legislative action that will go far beyond the v-chip venturing into the constitutional quagmire of "safe harbor" resolutions. What hangs in the balance is nothing more than the First Amendment. The v-chip is program neutral. But parents want the First Amendment to work for them as well as for the industry which often hides behind free speech protections and threats of protracted lawsuits as delaying tactics in responding to any means that would decrease violence on television. [On March 12, 1998, the FCC approved the TV parental guidelines, a ratings system that was designed for the v-chip.]

Today, the National PTA has sent *A Call to Action* to its over 28,000 local PTA units around the country. The mailing includes information about the FCC v-chip comment period with a request that the industry include content descriptors as part of the rating icon on the screen and in TV periodicals. For the National PTA, I am the least important person here. The really important people are the parents and our grassroots that have been speaking loudly and clearly about their preference for a content rating system, and it will be our grassroots that will appeal to Congress for further redress if the industry turns yet another deaf ear. Parents want to be able to make the program decisions themselves, and they want a rating system that will help them do this. There are very few issues in our organization that have the grassroots resonance and interest as does the quality of children's television and concerns over the violence, sexual content and adult language in TV programming.

Question Number 1: Parental Involvement

The National PTA and the industry have been trying to work out issues of children's programming for many years. I am not the first PTA leader to come before the Congress, but one of a procession of many National PTA representatives as far back as the 1930's who have petitioned Congress and the regulatory agencies about the need for quality television programming for their children and families. The National PTA has been at the forefront of these issues ever since, pushing for the creation of the Federal Communications Commission in 1933, monitoring and protesting deceptive advertising on radio and television aimed at children, advocating in favor of the Television Violence Act and the Children's Television Act, and urging a three hour minimum of children's television programming per week which we ultimately hope to convince the FCC to increase to one hour per day. Most recently, the National PTA supported the v-chip provisions of the Telecommunications Act of 1996 which is designed to provide information to parents so they are able to make better media choices for children.

> *"The v-chip can balance the industry's freedom to broadcast with the parent's right to choose."*

Even after 60 years of National PTA activism on these issues, hearings such as today's must be held to goad a resistant industry toward meeting their obligations to the public, and more specifically to children and families, as required by the Children's Television Act.

Let me remind this Committee that we are here today because voluntary self-regulation over the years and the Television Violence Act produced little results while parental frustration over increasing violence on television has escalated. Our preference has traditionally been to seek non-legislative solutions to children's television issues, but as industry resistance to parental concerns about violence on television has increased, so has parental pressure to use legislative vehicles in forcing the industry to reduce violent programming and increase educational options for families. In fact, parents have been extremely patient with the industry, and the v-chip has been proposed as the next step along an incremental continuum of pressure applied to an industry that has often responded to parents with violent programming, not better programming.

When the television industry agreed to establish a rating system and rate its programming, the National PTA asked to be part of the process as the ratings were being developed. In July of 1996, I met with representatives of the Television Ratings Implementation Group. The National PTA indicated its willingness to help make the ratings useful to parents, and even offered to sponsor parent focus groups in the fall of 1996 to ascertain the kind of ratings information parents needed. The National PTA wanted to work with the industry in seeking mechanisms that sought the input of parents, through objective, comprehensive, and independent means, so that the ratings would be consumer relevant, and not biased of either the National PTA or the industry's past positions. In essence, we wanted the parents who were going to use the ratings system to have a voice in the formation of "their" system, and we wanted to work with the industry in accomplishing this.

Unfortunately, the industry did not respond to our offer or our ideas. Because we believed that any position that the National PTA would take had to be based on our membership views, we joined with Dr. Joanne Cantor of the University of Wisconsin-Madison and the Institute for Mental Health Initiatives to devise and implement a survey, the results of which were released in November, 1996. Indeed, this approach was even broader and more definitive than our focus groups could have been. The information from the survey was communicated to Television Ratings Implementation Group the same day we released the information to the public and the media..

Obviously, the proposed ratings do not reflect the view of either the survey conducted by the National PTA or those conducted by the *U.S. News & World Report* of September 9, 1996, or the Media Studies Center/Roper Center poll of December 12, 1996—all of which indicate that parents want a ratings system that gives them comprehensive, objective details about programs so they can make informed decisions about what to watch. Why?

1. Parents believe that they can make a better decision about what their children should watch than the industry.

2. Children develop differently, and are very different at the same ages.

3. Not all parents care about the same things. Some parents may have concerns about language, some don't. Or, they may wish to have information about the types and frequency of violence on a program.

An age-specific system simply does not get the job done.

Question Number 2: Insufficient Ratings

The proposed industry rating system does not provide sufficient information so that parents can make the best programming decisions for their children, and the National PTA is asking the FCC to reject a system that is age-based only. In addition, the FCC should accept no rating system that does not include content icons on the TV screen such as V (for violence), S (for sexual depiction and nudity) and L (for adult language). Some cable networks, including Home Box Office, Cinemax, and Showtime already have their own codes or provide at least minimal descriptive information about violence, sex, and language. In addition, the industry's existing rating descriptions for each of the categories are confusing and insufficient. Their descriptors mix violence, language and sex and are too general to provide useful guidance for parents. Parents want to know the nature of the offending material, and how much there is and how graphic it is.

"Parents want to to able to make the program decisions themselves, and they want a rating system that will help them do this."

In addition, the National PTA is requesting that the FCC adopt the following for a valid ratings system:

1. A v-chip band that is broad enough that would allow parents to receive more than one rating system. Although this issue is covered in another set of

regulatory proceedings, it is complementary to the amount of information that parents have access to in determining their watching venue.

2. A rating icon on the screen that is larger, more prominently placed on the screen, and appears more frequently during the course of the program.

3. A rating board that is independent of the industry and the FCC, and that the board include parents. Currently, the industry rates itself which is a conflict of interest. The producers could hardly be an impartial audience, or capable of providing consistent and impartial information.

> *"Industry resistance to parental concerns about violence on television has increased."*

Lastly, in this current period when FCC is requesting comments to aid its decision-making responsibilities, and the industry is seeking public opinions itself, the National PTA recommends that the industry work with parents and advocacy organizations to fund an independent research study comparing their age-based system with a content-based system, such as HBO's to determine which better meets the needs of parents. After the study is conducted, the various stakeholders in this issue should convene to review the study and make final recommendations to the FCC based on the study results.

Question Number 3: Developing a Useful System

I cannot answer why other ratings systems were not selected. That is for the industry to answer and provide insights. We do acknowledge that the industry has made an effort to develop ratings, which the Television Ratings Implementation Group is quick to remind us they did not have to do. They have maintained that their ratings efforts were voluntary and they did not have to recommend a ratings system at all, according to the Telecommunications Act of 1996. So to the extent they proposed a ratings system, we thank the industry. The questions that need to be posed to the industry are: will they be willing to engage in an independent research study comparing an age-based system with a content-based system, and will they be willing to change their proposed ratings on the basis of that study.

In addition, the National Cable Television Association with Cable in the Classroom and the National PTA have been working cooperatively over the past several years in the *Family and Community Critical Viewing Skills Project*. This cooperative effort is designed to provide parents and teachers throughout the country with information and skills to help families make better choices in the television programs they watch, and to improve the way they watch these programs. We are tremendously proud of this project and relationship. To complement this project with a content-based ratings system would be such an effective merger between parental responsibility to develop better TV watching skills and the TV industry's responsibility of providing good information to enhance these skills.

We are on the verge of providing a useful tool to parents and we can't miss this opportunity of doing it right. Once a ratings system is institutionalized, it will be difficult, if not impossible, to revise. A lot is at stake—information for parents, no First Amendment restrictions on programming for the industry, and a private-public initiative that requires minimal government interference to protect the public interest. Or going about the old way of doing things.

The Regulation of Art Threatens Artistic Freedom

by David C. Mendoza

About the author: *David C. Mendoza is the former executive director of the National Campaign for Freedom of Expression.*

Institutional censorship has had an impact on artists and cultural groups producing work considered at or outside the margins of "mainstream" society. Publishing houses, foundations, record companies, art galleries, movie studios, and museums have historically been controlled by Caucasian men who haven't always been welcoming to artists of color, women, or out gays and lesbians. National Campaign for Freedom of Expression (NCFE) has been an active participant in public policy discussions, educational forums, and the media, educating the public about and advocating for continued progress toward eliminating institutional censorship.

At the end of the twentieth century, support for artists and cultures outside the mainstream has vastly improved. One precipitating factor of this change is also at the root of the threats to freedom of artistic expression today: public funding for culture.

The Growth of Public Funding

In 1965, President Lyndon Johnson signed legislation authorizing the National Endowment for the Arts and Humanities. Since then public funding for the arts and humanities has expanded, and today there are arts agencies in every state and territory, and in hundreds of county and municipal governments. There are also humanities commissions or councils in every state. Taxpayers have been serving as patrons of the arts and humanities for over thirty years.

With this public support came the imperative to recognize the rich artistic diversity of the people, cultures, and communities that make up America. Nonprofit organizations and artists that had never been the beneficiaries of philanthropy received not only financial support but also the imprimatur of respected public agencies such as the National Endowment for the Arts. This respect was

Excerpted from David C. Mendoza, foreword to *NCFE Handbook to Understanding, Preparing for, and Responding to Challenges to Your Freedom of Artistic Expression*. Reprinted with permission from the National Campaign for Freedom of Expression.

conferred by the peer panel process through which arts professionals adjudicate and award grants of public dollars to their peers. This process is a singular and powerful contribution to cultural democracy in America. There has been far more diversity in the NEA peer panels than in the Congress that has recently derided them. Peer panels—which change with each round of grant requests— have served to insulate the grantmaking process from political pressure by elected officials and even, to a large extent, by the members of the granting commissions appointed by the president, governors, and mayors.

> *"Since 1989 the arts community has faced an escalating attack on freedom of artistic expression."*

Public funding of the arts and humanities has been a key factor in the diversification of American cultural life. This move to diversify support for arts programs was a political imperative for public agencies because the money is contributed by all taxpayers, who could expect (unlike in corporate or private philanthropy at the time) to be represented on the staffs, panels, and appointed commissions, as well as in the organizations that received public funding. Slowly but steadily, these agencies have nurtured cultural expression reflecting a far broader range of national experience than was generally portrayed before 1960. The rise of public arts funding took place concurrently with the rise of the civil rights, women's, and gay and lesbian rights movements. As a result, we now can enjoy a rich gumbo of cultural and personal artistic expressions that did not exist before 1960. Ballet Hispanico (New York City), Northwest Asian American Theatre (Seattle), San Francisco Gay and Lesbian Film Festival, Black Theatre Festival (North Carolina), California Indian Basketweavers Association, and Women Make Art (Austin) are a tiny sampling of the organizations that have received public funding from the NEA and local arts agencies. A list of individual artists who have received public support would yield a similar diversity. The culture of America has finally begun to "look like America." Multiculturalism is neither rhetoric nor a political position; it is a reality as we move into the next millennium.

Attacks Against Art

Perhaps inevitably, there was a backlash from those who felt threatened by a multicultural America. Since 1989 the arts community has faced an escalating attack on freedom of artistic expression. In the spring of that year Robert Mapplethorpe (a gay photographer whose work included images of sadomasochism) and Andres Serrano (a photographer of Afro-Caribbean descent whose Piss Christ featured a plastic crucifix in a jar of urine) became the first targets in what has become known as the culture war. First denounced by the then little-known "religious right," these "blasphemous" and transgressive images—some presentations of which were funded in small part by public tax dollars—presented a significant political opportunity for

Senator Jesse Helms (R-NC) and his conservative cohorts.

The established arts community did not exactly leap to the front lines to defend against these broadsides from the right. Some thought the controversy would "blow over" quickly, others felt that the Mapplethorpe and Serrano works were too difficult to defend, and still others did not wish to risk their own funding to champion art at the margins. The silence of mainstream cultural organizations was, in fact, as deafening as the cries of outrage from the other side. In the face of the controversy, the Corcoran Gallery in Washington, D.C., canceled the Mapplethorpe exhibit because the gallery feared funding reprisal from Congress. That decision revealed an arts establishment vulnerable to attack. The fault lines were clear.

In response to this leadership vacuum, the National Campaign for Freedom of Expression was created in 1990 by artists, arts activists, and administrators of the organizations who had supported, produced, and presented the works of artists under attack. Support also came from funders and colleagues in the civil liberties community who had a history of supporting cultural diversity and fighting censorship. One of the first actions of NCFE was to initiate a lawsuit against the NEA in 1990 on behalf of four artists (John Fleck, Karen Finley, Holly Hughes, and Tim Miller) whose grants had been denied by then–NEA chair John Frohnmayer from fear of a Congressional funding reprisal. Several months later the suit was amended to include a constitutional challenge to the "standards of decency" clause which Congress included

> *"The war on the arts and culture is really a war on critical thinking, dissent, risk-taking, creativity, and democracy."*

in the reauthorization language of the NEA. Part of the suit was settled out of court in 1993 in favor of the four artists whose grants were reinstated. A federal district court ruled the "decency" language unconstitutional in 1992, and the Clinton administration appealed that decision. An appeals court upheld the district court ruling in November 1997. The administration appealed to the Supreme Court which heard the case in March 1998. A ruling is expected in June 1998. [The Supreme Court reversed the ruling.]

One unfortunate result of the court ruling against the "standards of decency," was that the chair and members of the NEA's National Council on the Arts learned to publicly talk about "artistic merit" when, in fact, their real concern was still the content. Although NEA spokespersons claimed otherwise, recorded transcripts of an August 1994 meeting of the council revealed that a decision to reject fellowships in photography for Andres Serrano, Barbara DeGenevieve, and Merry Alpern (fellowships that had been recommended by the peer panel) was motivated by concerns that there might be further political problems because of the content of the work. Council members also wanted to signal irate members of Congress that the NEA was paying attention to their outrage.

Chapter 4

Artistic Freedom Has Been Threatened

A rise of less well publicized challenges to artistic freedom has occurred throughout the nation. . . . Artistic freedom is threatened by well-intentioned arts officials who have grown nervous about potential controversy. It is not uncommon for an exhibit director to ponder the selection of a particular work of art based on its potential for generating controversy rather than on its artistic merit. Arts organizations valiantly defend freedom of expression in the face of a controversial program, and afterwards artistic directors or curators are warned by board members or funders "to be careful" in the future. And many artists, fearing they will not get a grant or commission or will be excluded from an exhibition, submit work they think conforms to some vague notion of decency standards. The true chilling effect of censorship is self-censorship. Danilo Kis, the late Czech writer, wrote in *HomoPoeticus* (1985):

> Invisible but here, far from the public eye and buried deep in the most secret parts of the spirit, [self-censorship] is far more efficient than censorship. While both depend on the same means—threats, fear, blackmail—self-censorship masks, or at any rate does not reveal the exercise of, constraint. The fight against censorship is open and dangerous and thus heroic, while the battle against self-censorship is anonymous, lonely, and unwitnessed—a source of humiliation and shame for the collaborator. Self-censorship means reading your own text through someone else's eyes, a situation that makes you your own judge. You become stricter and more suspicious than anyone else could, because you know what no censor could ever discover—your most secret, unspoken thoughts. . . .

The war on the arts and culture is really a war on critical thinking, dissent, risk-taking, creativity, and democracy. With disinformation, sound bites, and defamation of character, conservatives have demonized artists, transforming them in the public mind into blasphemers and pornographers. Ironically, many of the artists who have been defunded and defamed for being immoral are in fact communicating a moral vision. It is just that their art, appropriately—though disparagingly—labeled "political," is critical, unflinching, and often dissenting against the majority.

Often all it takes for a piece of art to be censored is for one person to complain that he or she finds it offensive. It has become almost a criminal act to offend someone. Expressing criticism of a controversial work—often without even seeing it—is not enough for some people; because they are offended they don't want anyone else to have access to the art. Perhaps they fear others will be offended. Perhaps they think others should be offended. But offending and dissenting are not only permissible but should be celebrated in a democratic society.

The great Japanese filmmaker Akira Kurosawa said, "Being an artist means never to avert one's eyes." I believe our challenge is not to avert our eyes from what artists see. And even if our religious or political beliefs compel us to avert our eyes we must, in a democracy, resist the urge to enforce our choice on others.

The Music Industry Can Regulate Itself

by Hilary Rosen

About the author: *Hilary Rosen is the president and chief executive officer of the Recording Industry Association of America.*

In 1956 the attention of America was largely directed at a singer whose gyrations that year led Ed Sullivan to call him "unfit for a family audience."

In 1997, there are those who think Elvis Presley is still around.

On this the recording industry is neutral.

Repeated Arguments Against Popular Music

But we see a similarity in the attacks on Elvis and those on contemporary music that lead us to this hearing today.

For much of this century, whether Ragtime or Rhythm and Blues or Rap, each generation has seen adults who compare it to the music of their youth and say, "This is different."

For good reason.

Popular music, after all, has often become the vehicle for young people to express the ways they differ from their parents.

While we approve of any forum focusing on the serious and real problems faced by today's young people, we passionately believe that most of the attacks on the lyrics of the 1990s should be categorized with those of the alarmed parents of 1950s teenagers in love with Elvis.

For that reason I'm particularly grateful to you, Mr. Chairman, for allowing us to speak this morning.

We share your concern. We are alarmed by the pervasive presence of drugs and violence in American culture and in the lives of young people.

In an America where each day 3 children die from child abuse, 15 die from guns, and 1,340 teenagers give birth, who could be indifferent to such problems? Certainly, we are not.

Excerpted from testimony given by Hilary Rosen before the U.S. Senate Committee on Governmental Affairs, Subcommittee on Oversight of Government Management, Restructuring, and the District of Columbia, November 6, 1997.

The Good Deeds of the Music Industry

We are involved in an industry important to young people. We are parents, too.

To read a letter like the one this Committee has from Mr. and Mrs. Kuntz is to be reminded of how precious our children's lives are—and how vulnerable. [The Kuntz's letter told of their son's suicide and their belief that a Marilyn Manson song led to that act.]

This sensitivity animates our work to fight drugs, promote good citizenship and end violence.

It is a concern shared by many of the artists being criticized here today and known only by the characters they play onstage.

You see this in Heavy D's involvement in "Operation Unity" promoting racial harmony in America's cities . . . Ice Cube's non-profit Brotherhood Crusade to aid the homeless and elderly . . . Queen Latifah's "Daddy's House" providing educational opportunities for underprivileged children.

In fact, I just returned from Los Angeles, where the Recording Industry Association of America (RIAA), the Musician's Assistance Program, the Partnership for a Drug Free America, and several recording artists launched a PSA campaign to urge young people to stay away from drugs. These PSA's will get nationwide exposure on MTV and other outlets and will continue throughout the year.

> *"In a retail record store with 110,000 titles, less than one-half of one percent of that store's total inventory will carry the Parental Advisory logo."*

It was a small part of our effort.

To us, success is not just measured in hit records. It is Joey, a learning disabled kid at the Nordoff Robbins-Center for Music Therapy in New York; it's Eduardo Garcia, a 12-year-old learning to read at Rosie's Garage in La Habra California, supported by Walt Disney Records; or Malika Roberson, scholarship winner in the World of Expression program created by BMG Entertainment.

Probably the most visible such effort—at least in Washington—is our Rock The Vote campaign, which registered millions of young people in 1992 and 96. One should look at why so many of those young people did not vote in the most recent election even after we registered them but perhaps that is the subject for a whole other hearing.

The music community is making a positive difference in many ways that don't get much attention.

Giving Parents Information

This by no means implies that our artists are perfect—or that all performers are singing gospel.

There are songs I wouldn't want a ten-year-old to hear anymore than I would want them to see scenes from *Chain Saw Massacre*, or *NYPD Blue*.

And it is precisely because the recording industry realizes that many Americans are genuinely concerned about the music their kids are listening to that we label our products.

We began in 1985.

We labelled records with a "Parental Advisory" sticker so parents could make intelligent listening choices for their children. When some said it wasn't visible enough, we did more.

Today, record companies are vigilant in applying those stickers. Indeed, it is ironic that every one of the albums being attacked here today, including Marilyn Manson and Snoop Doggy Dog, has been affixed with the "Parental Advisory" label.

> *"It is precisely because the recording industry realizes that many Americans are genuinely concerned about the music their kids are listening to that we label our products."*

But that's not all. We support efforts to have retailers restrict sales of albums to consumers under the age of 17. We believe that decision should be left to parents.

Give parents information? We agree.

Don't sell to minors? We agree.

And we don't stop there.

We have a consumer awareness campaign to enlighten parents about the Parental Advisory Program.

Lyrics Are Not Dangerous

For all of that, let's put this issue in perspective. In a retail record store with 110,000 titles, less than one-half of one percent of that store's total inventory will carry the Parental Advisory logo.

Just look at this week's *Billboard* Top 20. It reflects a culture more musically diverse than any culture in the history of the world.

In fact, Number 1 in *Billboard* last week was LeAnn Rimes' remake of the Debbie Boone hit "You Light Up My Life."

If young people are so influenced by music lyrics, we're in good shape.

Now, I must do something that both saddens me and makes me personally uncomfortable. I would prefer not to disagree with a loving parent like Mr. Kuntz, who has suffered the unendurable loss of his son, Richard.

The most controversial lyrics in popular music certainly reflect the violence of our culture. In some cases they mock the violence and drug use in ways that have been misinterpreted. In others, it is clear that performers are portraying a character—describing society—rather than preaching a message. But medical studies have concluded that while music may echo an adolescent's emotional state, it is not the cause of it. The American Academy of Child and Adolescent Psychiatry lists 14 signs to look for in a suicidal child. Music choices are not among them.

We don't think Marlon Brando is a Godfather. We don't think James Earl Jones really wants to turn people to the "dark side." Why believe any differently when we're listening to contemporary music?

For those who are sincerely offended by any music, the remedy is clear.

Read the labels.

If your child comes home with a CD, read the lyrics.

In this, we stand with mainstream America, 94% of whom agree it is the responsibility of parents to monitor the type of music their children listen to.

The Choices That Record Companies Make

Members of this committee should know that it is not an easy decision to sign an artist and release a record. The reason a record company invests in an artist is because the company believes that the artist has a unique vision and a creative way to express it. Music is not just about the lyrics. It is about the melody and the rhythm, combined with an expression of the soul that allows an artist or a band to capture the essential moments of understanding and mood. People respond to an artist's expression but music is a connection, not a directive.

Record company executives constantly make choices to not put out certain songs or albums because they don't meet the test of artistic credibility. But, for record companies to unilaterally deny opportunity to an artist with a difficult message is to deny that there are some in our society who express pain or anger in a way that is valuable, musical, and adds to our nation's cultural diversity of talent.

Why would we want to stifle the very voices that give us so much insight into the diversity of issues facing our young people? Shouldn't we listen more carefully instead of trying to turn off the music?

> *"It would be hypocritical to say artists can speak what they want—but deny their access to people who would listen."*

A determination to shut down the voices would be doomed to failure.

We are not a monolithic industry.

As long as there is an audience demanding to listen, there will be people willing to produce artists far outside the mainstream.

Which is as it should be.

Censorship Is Not the Solution

I fully understand those who with utter sincerity feel differently. But remember: at other points in history the critics were equally sincere. Art is subjective. And that is why America has wisely given free expression such latitude.

After all the test of whether America allows free speech is not whether it grants freedom to those with whom we *mildly* disagree. It is whether we grant it to those whose views—and language—make us apoplectic.

And to grant freedom of speech but deny the means of being heard? That's censorship as well, and a dangerous course. Most record companies take pride in the diversity of their rosters. It would be hypocritical to say artists can speak what they want—but deny their access to people who would listen. America has fought that battle before. We know that to allow speech but not the platform is not only to start down a slippery slope—it's to plunge off the edge of a cliff.

Teenagers Need Help and Understanding

I'd like to close this morning where we may be able to find common ground. We agree that young people today are worth investing in.

They need our help. There is a generation of teenagers out there who are crying out for respect, understanding and leadership. They are smarter than we give them credit for. They have an inherent belief that this is a wonderful time to be alive. Most of them, that is. Others have more despair. Violence in their schools or in their homes, the high cost of education and the pervasiveness of drugs and violence in society scares them. Recording artists have a unique ability to reach them in a positive way. This committee can be the start of a new dialogue with artists and young people. One that appreciates their unique bond and offers you an opportunity you don't normally have to participate in a positive discussion about the future of young America.

That's what I hope comes out of today's hearing.

Let's make sure that 40 years from now, when the controversial singers of today are remembered with the nostalgia we—or some of us—remember Elvis . . . that people say we reacted not just with fear but with foresight . . . not just with hysteria but with hope . . . not just with slander but with solutions.

Thank you.

The Music Industry Regulations Are Inadequate

by Charlie Gilreath

About the author: *Charlie Gilreath is the publisher of* Family Entertainment Guide.

Thank you for having me here today. This is a subject I have long thought important. From the start, I would like my comments to be considered not in the context of restricting adults' freedom of speech, but rather in consideration of a potential threat to children and young people.

Music Has Changed

Although music and entertainment have long been considered controversial, two dramatic changes have taken place over the last decade that must be addressed. Firstly, provocative images of violence and sex are reaching younger and younger children. Secondly, there is a new and significantly more troubling aspect to the violence portrayed in some music that makes this a serious social problem. While music once inspired introspection and personal experimentation, the consequences of that experience were borne by the individual. However today's music commonly glamorizes violence and aggression towards others, often innocent "victims." This creates a social problem—the effects of which we are realizing daily. It is widely accepted that music and entertainment played a significant role in inspiring the evolution from the values of the 50's into the sex, drugs and rock & roll of the 70's and 80's. However, it is often the same voices that reminisce with nostalgia on music's role in past social change, who will not accept entertainment's current role in the celebration of sex, violence and aggression, which are a part of today's culture.

My background is in the music industry. For over 15 years I have worked with numerous artists, record companies and publishers and gave little thought to the actual message music was sending children. Three years ago my engagement made me responsible for two children aged 8 and 11. As an adult, I had long forgotten the attention and interest children have in the details of music. The image

Excerpted from testimony given by Charlie Gilreath before the U.S. Senate Commerce Committee, June 16, 1998.

of the artist, their lyrics and ideas are being studied, memorized, and absorbed by kids—shaping their images of life just as it had generations before us. A few years ago these images began to leap from the artist works of fantasy—to the nightly news' recital of facts. Living in L.A., the relation between music and the escalation of violence seemed far too real. As gang violence peaked, gangster rap records were topping the charts. While marijuana use amongst teens was once again exploding, so was its popularization in more and more hit records and artist persons. I attended youth meetings and other events at which young people were making it clear that their problems with the law were an outgrowth of role modeling popular heroes—the same role modeling that had driven me as a teenager to believe and conform to the attitudes of my time. The influences of television, music and films are not subtle, they are obvious.

> *"Today's music commonly glamorizes violence and aggression towards others."*

It is ironic that we all question whether or not the extreme violence in films and entertainment today has an effect on our kids, and then shake our heads and wonder why our children are shooting their classmates.

It was clear to everyone that music was influencing our culture, from the inner-city to suburbia. As the violence increased, we thought the industry would take some action to address the obvious issues. Everyone knew that boundaries were being tested particularly where young children were concerned and yet rather than get proactive, to preserve their rights, they tried to ignore the problem. Once it was clear that the industry was not going to acknowledge the issue, I and others within my company created a publication called the *Family Entertainment Guide*. Because of our unbiased informative stance, we expected industry cooperation. What we found, however, was denial and fear. Denial of the problem which would never reach their privileged lives and "fear" of losing a cash cow if parents got hold of our information. So we are here today to look further at a problem that has a very simple solution.

Let me give you some quick facts and personal insights into the music industry that others may not be willing to give you.

Record Companies Are Focused on Money

Many top record company executives privately share your concerns about the content of music, yet will not interfere with what looks good on the bottom line. Music and entertainment are created in a unique culture that is often driven by a very young staff, interested only in the values important to their peers. Many senior executives would prefer that their labels stay away from this form of music, but again senior executives are driven by a bottom line that feeds fat salaries—not hundreds of thousands, but million dollar salaries often with significant bonuses. Take for example two key figures. Doug Morris, who worked with Interscope at Time Warner, received tens of millions of dollars in bonuses and severance pay upon his departure to MCA, and a recent partner in Priority Records (an independent label known for gangster rap) sold his interest to EMI for over $30 million.

Ironically if you look at the majority of rappers and rockers their fleeting fortunes are gone just a few short years after their success. I wonder sometimes if these artists understand how they and their culture are being exploited.

That said, keep in mind that these independent and major labels did not create these records in a vacuum. They have obviously tapped into a need or point of interest in our culture. This is not the case of an industry foisting upon the public something it does not want. As a matter of fact, the major labels were late on the gangster rap scene, and it was the independent record companies who rose from garages and dorm houses to become multimillion-dollar success stories. It was the independents' success in an area in which a major could not compete, that drove the majors' acquisition of rap and hard rock labels and acts.

It is a known fact that stickers do not work. The Recording Industry Association of America's (RIAA) and National Association of Recording Musicians's (NARM) own studies show that most parents do not know what a sticker means. The irony is that the kids who do know what these labels mean, treat them like a badge of honor. The film industry has learned from the Motion Picture Association of America (MPAA) experience that an R and PG rating has value at the box office. Kids and teens will not go to G-rated films. Around the world, music content and America's export of violent entertainment is an issue. In Australia there are three levels of stickers. In Germany over 100 groups are currently banned for content and in the U.K. video sales of *The Exorcist* are still banned.

> *"It is a known fact that [parental advisory] stickers do not work."*

Industry sales reports show that rap and hard rock sells to younger teens, and has little appeal to adults. Most marketing directors, let alone psychologists, agree that the more profane, base and exploitative messages appeal to the younger and more immature minds.

Marketing Music

In fairness, recently things have changed. Since the efforts of Dr. [Delores] Tucker, Senator [Joseph] Liebermann and Mr. [William] Bennett, along with others here, I have had projects at record companies where they have shown concern over the content of the records and have refused to sign exploitative artists.

However in general the record industry is aware of music's shock value and the power of shock content, and they exploit it for all it's worth. A full-page article in *Rolling Stone* magazine lauding a hot new artist for their hard-core antics sells more records than any full-page ad ever could. The bonus is that while you have to pay for an ad, an article is free, and one good article inspires more play on radio, print and powerful word-of-mouth promotion. Any marketing director at a major label will tell you that this is the way to create an artist's persona, build a career, and sell records. I have sat in major label meetings where the A&R people have stated that a record was "not controversial enough." Shock sells, and it sells best to teens—that is who our business targets. A billion-dollar industry has focused an awesomely powerful marketing machine on a segment of the population that is vulnerable and "in development."

Music is a unique form of entertainment we discover on our own, unlike film or television, which we start watching with our parents. This family aspect of T.V. and film gives parents some understanding and control over the childs' T.V. and film diet. However with music it is common for parents to react to their childrens' music by saying such things as "go to your room if you want to listen to that junk" or telling them to "turn down the noise." This sends kids and their music into a very isolated environment. Music defines the identity of many adolescents, and when children begin to define their own identity, it is the music that allows them to separate their identity from that of their parents—finding an affinity with other kids and explore new-found interests. If that area of interest is violent and angry, sexual or drug-oriented, so can be the influences. In the seventies "drug oriented music" glamorizing drug use was very popular, and in turn we had almost epidemic "youth drug culture." Which came first, the drug culture or the drug oriented music is irrelevant in light of the fact that, like today, one has begun to feed off the other. While we often hear the phrase, "we survived the 60's or the 70's," we should remember that many did not. With every Hendrix and Joplin, how many kids' lives were changed for the worse by what is now widely accepted as a failed social era?

Today, our pop culture environment is filled with lies and half-truths that popularize misleading images without showing the real consequences and long-term impact. Just as we feel that fine art has the ability to inspire great thought, and seek to expose our children to this, base expression or exploitative art also has inspirational abilities. The problem is that the people responsible for bringing fantasy into perspective—the parents and teachers—do have not the necessary resources or the influence over the children to combat the well funded marketing machine. Worst of all, those who could have an influence, do not have the necessary information to do so. Today's parents do not know what the music is saying or teaching. Ask a parent about their son or daughter's music, and they know very little.

> *"The record industry is aware of music's shock value and the power of shock content, and they exploit it for all it's worth."*

The rapid advancement of information access is a phenomenon from which our children will benefit only if we maintain free speech and freedom of expression. However, the power of new technology, coupled with the exploitative nature of the media today, is spoiling the party.

The information revolution is bringing more information to our children than ever before imaginable. While much of that information is thought to be educational, entertainment is in fact the driving factor in the development of these new technologies. Intel has stated time and again that new games and entertainment systems are driving demand and development of greater processor speed. As a result, younger children have access to more entertainment than ever before and yet parents know very little about what is coming into the home.

One Solution

When we first published the *Family Entertainment Guide,* many people in Washington were debating these issues and using our publication as a research resource. Everyone had concerns about entertainment content, and yet no one really had solutions. In fact, I was told that many politicians did not really want solutions, they just wanted to raise issues that would bring attention to themselves. I do not believe that, and yet I think we have talked a little too long about music and its influences on children, without any real dialogue regarding solutions.

Parents cannot abdicate their obligation to government and government cannot become the parent. We believe the solution is to empower parents with the information they

> *"The solution is to empower parents with the information they need to parent."*

need to parent. To the extent that government can insure parents have access to the information they need then that is what government can offer. Parents must be empowered to parent. No one knows better what is appropriate for a particular child than the parents.

The *Family Entertainment Guide* listens to and reviews the lyrics of all major releases, giving parents a simple unbiased synopsis and perspective from which to make informed decisions. Our information allows consumers to make informed decisions before purchasing. To this end, we are now using the information revolution to favor parents. Our reviews are currently linked to online and Internet retailers, enabling parents to listen to a sample of a record, read our parental reviews, and make an informed decision while shopping online. Further, as new forms of interactive media emerge, we are linking our reviews to television broadcasts of video, and can provide similar information over radio and through other forms of media. As the market develops for this form of information, parents and consumers will have a variety of viewpoints from which to choose. While the *Family Entertainment Guide* strives to maintain unbiased reviews, void of any religious perspective or social agenda, other parents may seek information from other sources. Varied information sources are available for parents today. *Entertainment Weekly* (a Time Warner publication) provides parental reviews of movies, and this section of their publication has been very popular. *Focus on the Family* and the Catholic church offer varying positions and reviews of music from a religious perspective, while Ted Bahr produces a Christian movie guide. Each one of these could be a valuable parental resource, but if you remember, when I opened, I said fear and anger met the launch of our magazine. This fear and anger have limited the development of this solution.

Retailers Are Frightened

Retail and record companies' fear and anger have impeded our information from reaching parents. Retailers refused to make it available, and the record companies will not support us in the same way as they support entertainment reviews which report from an aesthetic perspective. Ironically, it was the retailers who claimed to serve the family, such as Blockbuster, that were the most emphatic about not allowing this information in their store. This was out of fear of how their family consumer would react when informed about the records that these "family retailers" sell. We do not have the resources to break through this barrier, and need to have the playing field leveled.

The true industry fear is summed up in a analogy once made to me by a reporter: He said, "In the 60's, the seat belt was made available as an option. In the 70's, it was law that every car must provide them as standard equipment, and in the 80's, it become law that everyone must wear them. Now we have airbags, etc." He went on to ask, "By requiring this information, wouldn't we be standing on the doorstep of censorship?" My response was, by denying parents, educators and others our information aren't you engaging in censorship. I do not want censorship, yet I do not want to live in a world where we continue to glamorize ignorance and stereotype the races—playing to the basest elements of society just to turn a buck. I have faith in the public, and our system. Information brings understanding.

Despite the growing fears, the development of the information revolution may ultimately favor the family and empower parents provided we can ensure "equal information access." Once information is available, informed people will start to make intelligent choices, and those choices will change the market. Who knows? You may be surprised when you discover what rappers and rockers have to say. In the true spirit of our democracy and free market, those that have talent will gain a bigger voice, while the one-hit-wonders will simply fade away.

Bibliography

Books

Richard L. Abel	*Speaking Respect, Respecting Speech*. Chicago: University of Chicago Press, 1998.
Fred H. Cate	*The Internet and the First Amendment: Schools and Sexually Explicit Expression*. Bloomington, IN: Phi Delta Kappa Educational Foundation, 1998.
J.M. Coetzee	*Giving Offense: Essays on Censorship*. Chicago: University of Chicago Press, 1996.
Ronald K.L. Collins and David M. Skover	*The Death of Discourse*. Boulder, CO: Westview Press, 1996.
Francis G. Couvares, ed.	*Movie Censorship and American Culture*. Washington, DC: Smithsonian Institution Press, 1996.
Ann Curry	*The Limits of Tolerance: Censorship and Intellectual Freedom in Public Libraries*. Lanham, MD: Scarecrow Press, 1997.
Richard Delgado and Jean Stefancic	*Must We Defend Nazis?: Hate Speech, Pornography, and the New First Amendment*. New York: New York University Press, 1997.
Gail Dines, Robert Jensen, and Ann Russo	*Pornography: The Production and Consumption of Inequality*. New York: Routledge, 1998.
Richard Dooling	*Blue Streak: Swearing, Free Speech, and Sexual Harassment*. New York: Random House, 1996.
June Edwards	*Opposing Censorship in the Public Schools: Religion, Morality, and Literature*. Mahwah, NJ: L. Erlbaum Associates, 1998.
Stanley Eugene Fish	*There's No Such Thing as Free Speech, and It's a Good Thing, Too*. New York: Oxford University Press, 1997.
Owen M. Fiss	*The Irony of Free Speech*. Cambridge, MA: Harvard University Press, 1996.
Mike Godwin	*Cyber Rights: Defending Free Speech in the Digital Age*. New York: Times Books, 1998.

Censorship

Alan Haworth — *Free Speech*. London: Routledge, 1998.

Nat Hentoff — *Living the Bill of Rights: How to Be an Authentic American.* New York: HarperCollins, 1998.

Milton Heumann, Thomas W. Church, and David P. Redlawsk, eds. — *Hate Speech on Campus: Cases, Case Studies, and Commentary.* Boston: Northeastern University Press, 1997.

Steven J. Heyman, ed. — *Hate Speech and the Constitution.* New York: Garland, 1996.

Richard Klingler — *The New Information Industry: Regulatory Challenges and the First Amendment.* Washington, DC: Brookings Institution, 1996.

Alan Charles Kors and Harvey A. Silverglate — *The Shadow University: The Betrayal of Liberty on American's Campuses.* New York: Free Press, 1998.

David Lowenthal — *No Liberty for License: The Forgotten Logic of the First Amendment.* Dallas: Spence, 1997.

Charles Lyons — *The New Censors: Movies and the Culture Wars.* Philadelphia: Temple University Press, 1997.

Karen J. Maschke, ed. — *Pornography, Sex Work, and Hate Speech.* New York: Garland, 1997.

Brian McNair — *Mediated Sex: Pornography and Postmodern Culture.* London: Arnold, 1996.

William Nygaard, translated by Rosemary Fearn — *The Price of Free Speech.* Oslo: Scandinavian University Press, 1996.

Klaus Petersen and Allan C. Hutchinson, eds. — *Interpreting Censorship in Canada.* Toronto: University of Toronto Press, 1997.

Louise S. Robbins — *Censorship and the American Library: The American Library Association's Response to Threats to Intellectual Freedom, 1939–1969.* Westport, CT: Greenwood, 1996.

Bruce W. Sanford — *Don't Shoot the Messenger: How Our Growing Hatred of the Media Threatens Free Speech for All of Us.* New York: Free, 1999.

Ted Schwarz — *Free Speech and False Profits: Ethics in the Media.* Cleveland: Pilgrim, 1996.

Nadine Strossen — *Defending Pornography: Free Speech, Sex, and the Fight for Women's Rights.* New York: Scribner, 1995.

James Weinstein — *Hate Speech, Pornography, and the Radical Attack on Free Speech Doctrine.* Boulder, CO: Westview, 1999.

Mark West — *Trust Your Children: Voices Against Censorship in Children's Literature.* New York: Neal-Schuman, 1997.

Betty Houchin Winfield and Sandra Davidson, eds.	*Bleep!: Censoring Rock and Rap Music*. Westport, CT: Greenwood, 1999.

Periodicals

William J. Bennett and C. DeLores Tucker	"Smut-Free Stores," *New York Times*, December 9, 1996.
Eric Boehlert	"Culture Skirmishes," *Rolling Stone*, August 21, 1997.
Ethan Bronner	"Big Brother Is Listening," *New York Times Education Life*, April 4, 1999.
Mary Schmidt Campbell	"Collisions at a Museum," *Nation*, November 22, 1999.
Richard Delgado	"Q: Do Prohibitions of Hate Speech Harm Public Discourse? No: Such Rules Make Campuses and Workplaces User-Friendly to All," *Insight*, June 24, 1996. Available from 3600 New York Ave. NE, Washington, DC 20002.
Jim D'Entremont	"Preachers of Doom," *Index on Censorship*, July/August 1999.
Jim D'Entremont	"The Devil's Disciples," *Index on Censorship*, November/December 1998.
Dissent	"Minors and the First Amendment," Fall 1999.
Amitai Etzioni	"ACLU Favors Porn Over Parents," *Wall Street Journal*, October 14, 1998.
Paul Gottfried	"Q: Do Prohibitions of Hate Speech Harm Public Discourse? Yes: They Have a Chilling Effect on Scholarship and Freedom of Expression," *Insight*, June 24, 1996.
Mark Y. Herring	"X-Rated Libraries," *Weekly Standard*, July 5/July 12, 1999. Available from 1211 Avenue of the Americas, New York, NY 10036.
Marjorie Heins	"Screening Out Sex," *American Prospect*, July/August 1998.
Nancy Herzig and Rafael Bernabe	"Pornography, Censorship, Sexuality," *Against the Current*, March/April 1997.
Lester H. Hunt	"Repealing the Codes of Silence," *Liberty*, May 1999. Available from 1018 Water St., Suite 201, Port Townsend, WA 98368.
Issues and Controversies On File	"Internet Regulation Update," June 27, 1997. Available from Facts On File News Service, 11 Penn Plaza, New York, NY 10001-2006.
Issues and Controversies On File	"Television-Ratings Codes," February 21, 1997.

Censorship

Molly Ivins	"Even Racists Have Right to Free Speech," *Liberal Opinion Week*, September 29, 1997. Available from PO Box 880, Vinton, IA 52349-0880.
Charles Krauthammer	"The Mayor, the Museum, and the Madonna," *Weekly Standard*, October 11, 1999.
Gara Lamarche	"The Price of Hate," *Index on Censorship*, March/April 1999.
John Leo	"And the Winner Is . . ." *U.S. News & World Report*, October 13, 1997.
Maria Margaronis	"Purgation and Liberation," *Index on Censorship*, March/April 1999.
Barbara Miner	"Reading, Writing, and Censorship," *Rethinking Schools*, Spring 1998.
Nation	"Speech & Power," July 21, 1997.
Peggy Orenstein	"Censorship Follies, Town by Town," *New York Times*, December 7, 1996.
Randall E. Stross	"The Cyber Vice Squad," *U.S. News & World Report*, March 17, 1997.
Laurence H. Tribe	"The Internet vs. the First Amendment," *New York Times*, April 28, 1999.
Jacob Weisberg	"A Well-Staged Scandal," *New York Times Magazine*, October 10, 1999.
Julia Wilkins	"Protecting Our Children From Internet Smut: Moral Duty or Moral Panic?" *Humanist*, September/October 1997.

Organizations to Contact

The editors have compiled the following list of organizations concerned with the issues debated in this book. The descriptions are derived from materials provided by the organizations. All have publications or information available for interested readers. The list was compiled on the date of publication of the present volume; the information provided here may change. Be aware that many organizations take several weeks or longer to respond to inquiries, so allow as much time as possible.

American Civil Liberties Union (ACLU)
125 Broad St., 18th Floor, New York, NY 10004
(212) 549-2500 • fax: (212) 549-2646
e-mail: aclu@aclu.org • website: www.aclu.org

The ACLU is a national organization that defends Americans' civil rights guaranteed in the U.S. Constitution. It adamantly opposes regulation of all forms of speech, including pornography and hate speech. The ACLU offers numerous reports, fact sheets, and policy statements on a wide variety of issues. Publications include the briefing papers "Freedom of Expression," "Hate Speech on Campus," and "Popular Music Under Siege."

American Library Association (ALA)
50 E. Huron St., Chicago, IL 60611
(800) 545-2433 • fax: (312) 440-9374
e-mail: ala@ala.org • website: www.ala.org

The ALA is the nation's primary professional organization for librarians. Through its Office for Intellectual Freedom, the ALA supports free access to libraries and library materials. The OIF also monitors and opposes efforts to ban books. The ALA's sister organization, the Freedom to Read Foundation, provides legal defense for libraries. Publications include the *Newsletter on Intellectual Freedom*, articles, fact sheets, and policy statements, including "Protecting the Freedom to Read."

Canadian Association for Free Expression (CAFE)
PO Box 332 Station B, Etobicoke, ON M9W 5L3 Canada
(905) 897-7221
e-mail: cafe@canadafirst.net • website: www.canadianfreespeech.com

CAFE, one of Canada's leading civil liberties groups, works to strengthen the freedom of speech and freedom of expression provisions in the Canadian Charter of Rights and Freedoms. It lobbies politicians and researches threats to freedom of speech. Publications include specialized reports, leaflets, and *The Free Speech Monitor*, which is published ten times per year.

Concerned Women for America (CWA)
1015 Fifteenth St. NW, Suite 1100, Washington, DC 20005
(202) 488-7000 • fax: (202) 488-0806
website: www.cwfa.org

CWA is a membership organization that promotes conservative values and is concerned with creating an environment that is conducive to building strong families and raising healthy children. CWA publishes the monthly *Family Voice*, which argues against all forms of pornography.

Electronic Frontier Foundation (EFF)
1550 Bryant Street, Suite 725, San Francisco, CA 94103-4832 USA
(415) 436-9333 • fax: (415) 436-9993
e-mail: ask@eff.org • website: www.eff.org

EFF is a non-profit, non-partisan organization that works to protect privacy and freedom of expression in the arena of computers and the Internet. Its missions include supporting litigation that protects First Amendment rights. EFF's website publishes an electronic bulletin, *Effector*, and the guidebook *Protecting Yourself Online: The Definitive Resource on Safety, Freedom & Privacy in Cyberspace*.

Family Research Council (FRC)
700 13th St. NW, Suite 500, Washington, DC 20005
(202) 393-2100 • fax: (202) 393-2134
e-mail: corrdept@frc.org • website: www.frc.org

The Family Research Council is an organization that believes pornography degrades women and children and seeks to strengthen current obscenity law. It publishes the monthly newsletter *Washington Watch* and the bimonthly journal *Family Policy*, which features a full-length essay in each issue, such as "Keeping Libraries User and Family Friendly: The Challenge of Internet Pornography." FRC also publishes policy papers, including "Indecent Proposal: The NEA Since the Supreme Court Decency Decision," and "Internet Filtering and Blocking Technology."

Freedom Forum
1101 Wilson Blvd., Arlington, VA 22209
(703) 528-0800 • (703) 284-2836
e-mail: news@freedomforum.org • website: www.freedomforum.org

The Freedom Forum is an international organization that works to protect freedom of the press and free speech. It monitors developments in media and First Amendment issues on its website, in its monthly magazine *Forum News*, and in the *Media Studies Journal*, published twice a year.

Free Speech Coalition
P.O. Box 10480, Canoga Park, CA 91309
(800) 845-8503 or (818) 348-9373
e-mail: freespeech@pacificnet.net • website: www.freespeechcoalition.com

The coalition is a trade association that represents members of the adult entertainment industry. It seeks to protect the industry from attempts to censor pornography. Publications include fact sheets, *Free Speech X-Press*, and the report *The Truth About the Adult Entertainment Industry*.

International Freedom of Expression Exchange (IFEX)
The IFEX Clearing House
489 College St., Suite 403, Toronto, ON M6G 1A5 Canada
(416) 515-9622 • fax: (416) 515-7879
e-mail: ifex@ifex.org • website: www.ifex.org

IFEX consists of more than forty organizations that support the freedom of expression. Its work is coordinated by the Toronto-based Clearing House. Through the Action Alert Network, organizations report abuses of free expression to the Clearing House, which distributes that information throughout the world. Publications include the weekly *The Communiqué*, which reports on free expression triumphs and violations.

Morality in Media (MIM)
475 Riverside Dr., Suite 239, New York, NY 10115
(212) 870-3222 • fax: (212) 870-2765
e-mail: mim@moralityinmedia.org • website: www.moralityinmedia.org

Morality in Media is an interfaith organization that fights obscenity and opposes indecency in the mainstream media. It believes pornography harms society and maintains the National Obscenity Law Center, a clearinghouse of legal materials on obscenity law. Publications include the bimonthlies *Morality in Media* and *Obscenity Law Bulletin* and reports, including "Pornography's Effects on Adults and Children."

National Coalition Against Censorship (NCAC)
275 Seventh Ave., New York, NY 10001
(212) 807-6222 • fax: (212) 807-6245
e-mail: ncac@ncac.org • website: www.ncac.org

The coalition represents more than forty national organizations that work to prevent suppression of free speech and the press. NCAC educates the public about the dangers of censorship and how to oppose it. The coalition publishes *Censorship News* five times a year, articles, various reports, and background papers. Papers include "Censorship's Tools Du Jour: V-Chips, TV Ratings, PICS, and Internet Filters."

National Coalition for the Protection of Children & Families
800 Compton Rd., Suite 9224, Cincinnati, OH 45231-9964
(513) 521-6227 • fax: (513) 521-6337
website: www.nationalcoalition.org

The coalition is an organization of business, religious, and civic leaders who work to eliminate pornography. It encourages citizens to support the enforcement of obscenity laws and to close down neighborhood pornography outlets. Publications include the books *Final Report of the Attorney General's Commission on Pornography*, *The Mind Polluters*, and *Pornography: A Human Tragedy*.

People for the American Way (PFAW)
2000 M St. NW, Suite 400, Washington, DC 20036
(202) 467-4999 or 1-800-326-PFAW • fax: (202) 293-2672
e-mail: pfaw@pfaw.org • website: www.pfaw.org

PFAW works to promote citizen participation in democracy and safeguard the principles of the U.S. Constitution, including the right to free speech. It publishes a variety of fact sheets, articles, and position statements on its website and distributes the e-mail newsletter *Freedom to Learn Online*.

Index

Index

Jefferson, Thomas, 19, 27
John Paul II (pope), 67
Journalism Education Association, 125

Kaczynski, Ted, 28–29
Kalven, Harry, 86
Kaminer, Wendy, 50
Karim, Persis M., 61
Kimball, Roger, 132
Kis, Danilo, 147
Kors, Alan Charles, 54
Kristol, Irving, 97

Lee, Harper, 62
Levendosky, Charles, 41, 131
Lewis, C.S., 97
libels, 16, 19, 80
libraries
  and children, 63–65
  and *in loco parentis,* 107
  and Internet filters, 109, 124, 125, 126
  in prisons, 105–106
  role of, 110–13
  selection of materials for, 75–76, 109
Liebling, A.J., 12
Lolita (movie), 119
Lowenthal, David, 17
Lynn, Leon, 66

Madsen v. Women's Health Center, 49
Mapplethorpe, Robert, 135, 145, 146
Marshall, Robert, 105
Marshall, Thurgood, 92
Marx, Gary, 124–25
mass media. *See* entertainment industry
masturbation, 100
Mazur, Marilyn C., 114
McCain, John, 122
McVeigh, Timothy, 28
Meeks, Brock, 123
Melnick, Jim, 75
Mendoza, David C., 144
Metzger, Tom, 25
Milburn, Brian, 127
Mill, John Stuart, 19
Miller v. California, 39–40, 91–94, 115–16
Miner, Barbara, 122
Monkey Trial, 66, 68
Monteiro, Kay, 53
Montesquieu, Charles Louis, 55
moral pollution, 18
Morris, Henry, 68, 76, 77
music industry
  and culture
    influences, 156

reflects, 150, 151
  is a positive force among youth, 149
  is diverse, 150, 151
  is harmful, 153, 154
    con, 150, 151
  is motivated by profits, 154–55, 156
  self-regulation
    is effective, 149–50
    con, 155

NAACP v. Claiborne Hardware, 49
National Association for the Advancement
  of Colored People (NAACP), 49, 53
National Association of Biology Teachers,
  67, 72
National Campaign for Freedom of
  Expression, 146
National Center for Science Education, 69
National Endowment for the Arts (NEA),
  135, 144–45, 146
National Parent-Teacher Association
  (PTA), 138, 139–40
National Review (magazine), 13
national security, 38–39
natural selection, 67
New York Herald (newspaper), 53
New York Times (newspaper), 39
New York Times v. Sullivan, 27, 39, 80
New York v. Ferber, 116
Nichols, Stephen M., 16
nudity, 118–21
"Nuremberg Files" (website), 48, 50–51

obscenity
  and book banning, 62
    history of, 115
  and community standards, 91, 92, 93
  in entertainment, 18, 19, 20
  immoral libels as, 19
  on Internet, 20
  is not protected by First Amendment, 20,
    39–40
  nonsexual, 98
  nudity as, 118–21
  public sex, 98–99
  Supreme Court decisions about
    definitions of, 20, 91–92, 93–94,
      115–16
    minors access to, 116, 117
    possession of, 92, 93, 94
  variable, 117
  see also pornography
Of Pandas and People, 72

Pacifica Radio, 117

169

Index

171